52 Weeks to a Great New Life

52 Weeks to a
Great New Life

Richard H. Noonan

Parker Publishing Company, Inc.   West Nyack, N.Y.

Dedicated To: Those who seek—for they shall find
—a great new life,
—the means to achievement of their desires,
—prosperity, peace of mind, and health.

Library of Congress Cataloging in Publication Data

Noonan, Richard H
    52 weeks to a great new life.

    1. Self-realization. I. Title.
BJ1470.N66   248'.4   73-12033
ISBN 0-13-314872-6

Printed in the United States of America

What This Book Can Do for You

WHAT THIS BOOK CAN DO FOR YOU is stated in one sentence: What *you* do with it. "What *will* this book do for you?" is a question of paramount importance. *Nothing. Or—everything! It all depends on you.* This book comprises ways and means for personal development which can bring vast and dramatic changes in your life, as it has in the lives of many others following the programs in the book.

That is the purpose of this book, which came to be written as a result of four primary considerations:

One, continuing years of counseling with individuals from all walks of life made it ever more apparent that while many people do genuinely seek help with problems, and sincerely make an effort to do something constructive with life, all too many just do not know how.

Two, through the opportunity of touching the lives of others in a deep and meaningful way, insights were developed which could enrich and make more meaningful the life of every individual.

Three, the resultant effectiveness of a series of classes I taught in many parts of our country with the material presented here as the basis under a course of instruction entitled "Dynamics of Living."

Four, through the marked changes in the lives of those who applied the principles of the program, it was both evident and obvious that *all* men have far greater potential than they do the knowledge of *how* to turn potential into positive, productive, and creative living.

Nearly twenty-five hundred years ago one of the world's greatest philosophers, Socrates, said to a young man with a mind for the very best of life, a youth of brilliant promise, "Wisdom begins in wonder." As this is truth, another truth is: A life of fulfillment, productivity, creativity, good, happiness, and meaning begins with a program of governed living so that the individual has awareness that he is a pawn, not of fate, but of his own mind; that he can, as with a compass, set and chart his course through and to that kind of life. I recommend that for best results, you follow the programs in the order set out in the book. Divorce, alcoholism, anxiety, fear, the sense of failure, lack of meaning, purpose, direction—worth—are not challenges unique to those of lesser financial circumstance. The rich and successful, as do the failures, inherit the seed of misdirected thought.

With the first chapter the curtain rises on the drama of life. What to do about it is to develop an understanding of self in a program of consistently unfolding steps, arousing within the individual an excitement about the life that is beginning to unfold. The book, no longer a book, is a friend, counseling in time of need, giving inspiration and insight, guiding, directing, and pointing the way from where you have been to where you are—and where you are is where you have sought to be. As you progress, step by step, in the program in the order outlined, you will discover little in life antagonistic to you, for you will—in mind, memory, and possession—have ever at your side a trusted companion challenging you to be all that you were meant to be—and—more important—pointing out the way.

While we cannot recapture the past, we can and must live in the present. Each person has a share in the responsibility for his own future. This volume is an account of life and how it can be lived for the greatest satisfaction. In the simplest of language, what this book can do for you is what you do with it. Set up as a program of principled, purposeful living, each section introduces you to a new direction of thinking, bringing forth, *from you,* new energy, strength, ability to get what you desire from life.

Richard H. Noonan

Contents

Author's Note: This book is set up as a series of programs for your development. If you are inclined, peruse the various sections at random. However, to achieve the best results for your benefit, it is definitely intended that you take each step in chapter order.

Your Assignment for This Week 205
Your Daily Affirmation for the Week 206
Your Basis of Reality in Today's Living 206
Your Self-Development Questions 206
Stimulators to Action 207

Your Assignment for This Week 209
Your Daily Affirmation for the Week 209
Your Basis of Reality in Daily Living 210
Your Self-Development Questions 210
Stimulators to Action 211

Your Assignment for This Week 215
Your Daily Affirmation for the Week 216
Your Basis of Reality in Daily Living 216
Your Self-Development Questions 217
Stimulators to Action 218

Your Assignment for This Week 220
Your Daily Affirmation for the Week 220
Your Basis of Reality in Daily Living 221
Your Self-Development Questions 221
Stimulators to Action 222

Your Assignment for This Week 225
Your Daily Affirmation for the Week 226
Your Basis of Reality in Daily Living 226
Your Self-Development Questions 226
Stimulators to Action 227

How to Have an Expanded Consciousness for a Great New Life

These programs have one aim: results productive of *immediate* use of your mind and spirit to improve your life and help you lead the life you want to live. You are not presented with anything beyond your power. You are equipped to live a masterful, meaningful life. If you have not started to do this, it is never too late to begin. But you must begin where you are and in earnest. These programs or lessons are an encouragement and a method of instruction. It is necessary only to proceed. The results will prove the worth. No great demand is placed upon you—only a few moments of your time each day. Are you ready and willing? You are able! Your wanting this book says so!

Someone once asked, "Is the seeker different from the thing he seeks? Is the thinker different from the thought?" While the question may appear insignificant in its simplicity, it is profound in understanding. The implications are far reaching. A man without health would ostensibly seek health. He would also appear far removed from the thing he seeks. Reconsider the question: "Is the seeker different from the thing he seeks?" If he is *really* seeking health—*deeply, desperately, desiring well-being*—will these not be in the thoughts he has, the image he projects? In this, he is the thing he seeks.

The thinker is no different from the thought. To expand your mind, improve your affairs, understand God, relate in any way to anything, the thought, the idea, the concept, must first be within your mind. The thinker is no different from the thought. The seeker is no different from that which he seeks. As reluctant as we may be to recognize aim, object, and end, *and its final relationship*

17

*to our state of mind—there can be no transformation in body or
affairs until there is transformation within our minds.* An expansion of consciousness can take place as the result of a traumatic
experience, but a greater expression of all that is good results from
quiet, contemplative moments of meditation, precisely determined
by you in times set aside for "inner growth."

YOUR ASSIGNMENT FOR THIS WEEK

Today, this moment, now—is the only time you will ever have.
Tomorrow is for the one who would not do that which can be
done. Tomorrow is for him who is without interest. Where there is
interest there is activity and transformation. How beautifully he
who crucified the early Christians put it when he finally saw the
light: *"Be not conformed to this world, but be ye transformed by
the renewing of your mind, that you may prove what is that good
and acceptable and perfect will of God."—Romans 12:2.* Will you
accept the challenge and the change—and transform yourself?

The earnest person is the one who is completely dedicated to
the task at hand. There is a simplicity in that which we seek to
do—when we dedicate ourselves to the doing.

At this moment accept only that which uplifts. But do not
reject that which you do not understand or that to which you
have failed to relate. Seek to find in it that which uplifts. In a
definite change of attitude, embrace all things as part of you. And
then, release—all and everything.

Become still. Know that order, divine order, is the self,
expressed through an expanded conscious awareness of you, your
world, and *your* part in it.

Make no effort to determine the "how" or the "why." *Accept.
Relax. Release.* In this moment of quiet signification, there will be
enlargement of you, as an individual—all else and all others will
emerge in the light as of a new and brighter dawn.

Write down on paper that which has been enscribed upon your
heart.

"I will now say, Peace be within thee." —Psalm 122:8

EVEN AMONG THE WEALTHY WE FIND THE POOR

Such a man was J.T., who had a responsible position in a large manufacturing company. He owned extensive property, raised cattle as a profitable hobby, and had a wife and a beautiful family. With all this he was a most unhappy man. He stated, "I've got everything that a man could call good. And I've got much that is the envy of others. And yet, damn it—I'm miserable. The good that seems to have come my way has been through little effort on my part and as a result I neither feel a sense of accomplishment, worth, nor direction. I've tried to analyze why I should be miserable and I guess I'm just not dedicated to the task at hand—I really don't feel as though I have a goal in life."

He may not have known it but he had stated his own problem, and in the so doing had incorporated the one word best defining the solution: *goal.* Without a goal we all flounder. I asked him a question each of us may well ask ourselves, "Is the thinker any different from the thought?" What he had been thinking was that there was no challenge, no goal, no sense of dedication, and little sense of self-worth. At this time he had been thinking of and embracing *thought, and using the power of that thought to reduce everything that was of value in his life to less than its own worth.* The result? Lacking a goal, guidance, or direction, he devaluated everything in his life and his relationship to it. Though a rich man, he was truly poor—and he was miserable.

I asked him what advice he would give to another in a situation such as his—what he would, under similar circumstances, say to one of his own children. He thought for a time and then said, "I think I would suggest that another 'expand his consciousness, broaden his horizons, and look to the opportunities existing right then in his own world.' "

We proceeded to discuss patterns of thought that were within the reach of every individual—without exception. At that time I happened to be lecturing on "The Powers Within" and the "Dynamics of the Mind." J.T. attended this series, and began to be the beautiful example we read about: he would corner everyone and tell them of the changes that took place in his life and affairs—how everything just seemed to take on a different atmosphere once one knew of the potential and the power within, and then applied the principle of this power. He made a contract with himself to always have before him a new goal, and, as he said, *"The Really amazing part about the changes for the better and the appreciation of that which I not only have, but have to work with, is the fact that through what you have pointed out, I know I have "The Keys to the Kingdom," and I'm happy—really happy for the first time in my life."*

MAKE THIS—

YOUR DAILY AFFIRMATION FOR THE WEEK:

"I would know God. This I do in quiet contemplation. Each day this week, I set aside a moment for meditation. I observe, in deep consideration, all that I observe. I would know God, and thus I do know God!"

Your basis of reality in daily living

Each one of us can learn the truth, expand the consciousness, be transformed in spirit, soul, and body—evolve—in a thousand different ways. We can unfold, expand and develop by observation of the flowers of the field, the trees of the forest, the man, woman, or child encountered along the way. However, rather than by chance, unfolding a program patterned to "knowing" God and fellow man, the world in which we live, who we are, and why, is by far the better way.

Yes, we can find God, learn Truth, and know others and ourself. And this we can do by manner and means without end: revelation as infinite as a star-filled sky awaits us in seed and bee and bug and fleck of dust. But we must look and see and hear and feel—far beyond the blinding illumination of that which appears to be—to that which is. Know the following quotation as your daily working guide:

"I would know God. This I do in quiet contemplation. Each day this week, I set aside a moment for meditation. I observe, in deep

consideration, all that I observe. I would know God, and thus I do know God!"

Your self-development questions

Every human being is seeking the better things of life. How diligently he pursues that which he seeks is the determinant of his success or failure. The material presented now is a positive guideline in that search, and will, as a search of the self, conclude each discipline. While it is important to answer all the questions, there is no right or wrong answer in terminology. However there are right answers both in understanding and in application. Answer briefly and in the light of how you feel regarding the questions. *But for aid in your own development, do answer the questions.* This can be done in a notebook and kept for future reference and reconsideration.

Question 1. We live a drama of conflict. Endless possibilities for our betterment or detriment exist. An added challenge in the forces that shape and mold is that we are the determinant factor. *To what extent do you believe you determine your life and by what means?*

Question 2. Maturity is the same thing for you as it is for me. It is also the very same thing for every individual regardless of age or background; that is, intelligent action in any given situation. *What is the most significant factor in developing maturity and why have you selected this particular factor?*

Question 3. The building of a spiritually conscious expression of life requires much of an individual and gives more in return. Most of us believe we know what we should receive. *What is required, or rather, demanded of us?*

Question 4. The capacity to resist pressures, to lift ourselves up when life has laid us low, to "go it alone" may be fine if one has the desire, the inclination, and the tendency to accept life as a battering-ram. There is an easier and better way, not to eliminate life's difficulties, but to make them less difficult. *What is this way? If it is so practical, what makes it practical?*

"I will be as the dew unto Israel: he shall grow as the lily, and cast forth his roots as Lebanon." –Hosea 14:5

Case history of a
marriage saved

In the counseling profession, one soon becomes aware of the greatest joys and the deepest heartbreak of one's fellow man. Usually, in counseling, one learns of the great joys once they have turned to shattered dreams.

Such was the experience of this most attractive young lady who entered my office. A fashion model, a mother, and the wife of a successful businessman, she was the embodiment of heartbreak, a deeply desperate woman. "What can I do to save my marriage? I have tried everything everyone has told me—all to no avail." Tears flooded her eyes as she proceeded to share with me that which troubled her: Her husband's infidelity, his drinking, and his abuse. "What can I do? What can I do?" she begged.

Bordering on quiet hysteria, it was apparent that this young woman needed to more than save her marriage. Peace of mind and a sense of inner calm were absolutely essential. Talking to her husband indicated little interest on his part in contributing anything other than money to this marriage.

The psychology of mind dynamics *is* a powerful influence and became *the vital factor* in this young woman's life. In her desperation she told me, "I will do anything, anything to try to save my marriage." We spent nearly an hour in an exercise of mental and physical relaxation, the means of total release. At the end of the hour I beheld a far different woman from the one who first entered my office. Her first words to me at the end of the hour of counseling were, "I want to save my marriage—but—whatever comes I know I have the strength to face it now. Perhaps even more important, I realize that some of my attitudes may have contributed to my husband's action. I know now that always I am building, but—perhaps for the first time I know that the materials I use can be used for benefit or destruction.

Several weeks elapsed before I saw this young lady again. I asked her if she still had a marriage. With a smile she said, "Ask my husband, he's directly behind you." Turning, I knew the answer to the question I had just asked. Suntanned, they had just returned from a vacation together in the Islands!

"STIMULATORS TO ACTION"–

You seek to know and understand?
How deeply burns that fire within?
Take this
one thing you seek
to know—
Give thought to it and nothing else.
Hold tightly to it night and day
For just one day.
You will hold to it—forevermore!

WEEKLY PROGRAM
NUMBER
2

How to Select Building Materials for Your Great New Life

You are beginning a systematic practice structured to release potential. Your basic attitude must be one of constancy. The measurement of results is implicit in the effort expended. Begin with the discipline of daily practice of "a time of quiet." Promise: *"I will establish my covenant with thee." —Genesis 6:18*

THE POWER OF FAITH

To those not fully persuaded of the existence of something they can neither see, feel, nor touch, it could easily appear that the essence of spiritual teachings must be based on postulation without proof. This is not so. With the magnificent power of the mind, we are able to close our eyes, open our mind, heart and spirit and "see" things as they were at a time in the past. But with the vision of hope, aspiration, inspiration, and dreams we are able, in a very real sense, to "see" that which is yet to be, to unfold, and to come forth.

Can you accept that the building materials of your life and mine are the subtle influences of an unseen spiritual nature? We do not see the steel covered with concrete within a building, but it is there nonetheless. We may not see nor touch nor take within our hand the various materials with which we evolve and build a life: the emotion, the mind, and the spirit of love. We see that which emotion, mind, spirit, love, and all our attitudes have built.

In the course of your investigation consider:

"What can we know? or what can we discern,
When error chokes the windows of the mind?"
                    —Sir John Davies, *The Vanity of Human Learning*

And even more important:

"Look round the habitable world: how few
Know their own good, or knowing it, pursue."

                                              —Dryden, "Juvenal"

YOUR ASSIGNMENT FOR THIS WEEK

*Now — today—this moment—*Accept that great lives, great moments, great expressions and inspiration, have all been built with and through *that great unseen power,* and *"wrought not with human hands."* Know that this power is yours to do with as you will—but do with it you will—for good or ill.

Both the frailest of creatures and the strongest of men avoid that which would destroy them, yet neither pursues that which will give them life. Each expresses a desire for that which will sustain, and yet avoids this same sustaining power—one through inability, the other through failure to act each day, and each moment to build solid substance—life—from the building materials of mind, heart, and spirit.

"LISTEN!
—to the Exhortation of the Dawn!
Look to this Day! For it is Life,
The very Life of Life.
In its brief course lie all the
Verities and Realities of your Existence;
The Bliss of Growth,
The Glory of Action,
The Splendour of Beauty.
The Salutation of the Dawn!"
                                —"The Salutation of the Dawn"
                                (translated from the Sanskrit)

Application of truth:

"I can do all things *through* Christ which strengtheneth me."
                                                —Philippians 4:13

Read and meditate upon: The Epistle of Paul to the Colossians, Chapter 1. And again, know *of the potential perfection within each man: "I CAN DO ALL THINGS THROUGH CHRIST WHICH STRENGTHENETH ME!"* Spiritual values are spiritual—and of value—only when applied and incorporated into our lives.

MAKE THIS—

YOUR DAILY AFFIRMATION FOR THE WEEK:

"Spiritual realization of divine substance enriches me in a very real manner, in health of body, peace of mind, and in the material substance of prosperity."

**Your basis of reality
in daily living**

For centuries man has had ideas, concepts and prejudices concerning the character, quality, and makeup of his environment, his state of health, and the conditions of his affairs. A knowledge of the origin, a concept of the cause, and an understanding of that which is part and parcel of all we experience is essential if we would direct our life and affairs, rather than proceed as the oceans rise and fall, and toss to and fro like the chip upon the wave.

Beyond the sight or sound of our affirmation for the week lies a deeper meaning: "Spiritual realization of divine substance enriches me . . . " "Spiritual" in its reduction means "spirit," or "the inspiring principal dominant influence." "Realization" is "the deep inner conviction and assurance of the fulfillment of an ideal." "Substance" connotes "the divine idea (unlimited) of the underlying reality of all things."

"Spiritual realization of divine substance enriches me in a very real manner, in health of body, peace of mind, and in the material substance of prosperity."

Your self-development questions

The following questions are propounded to make you think—to question and understand yourself and the world in which you live and, more important, your part in it.

Question 1. Many intelligent and free-thinking people propound the question: *"How can any intelligent person believe in religion?"* To which most religionists (ministers, priests, rabbis) would answer, *"If a man does not yield himself to God, he yields himself to something less than God."* Any reasonably intelligent person can readily discern merit in both question and answer. *If you were asked the above question, how would you, reasonably intelligently, give an answer as to the importance and necessity of "yielding" to something beyond the self?*

Question 2. In the world around us we see many examples of people "without God" doing just fine—doing really well. *Why do they have the things that others may seek and never find through church, religion, and a religious way of life? Why do they seem to get along just fine without religion, God, or things of the spirit?*

Question 3. We can say that much that man does denies that God is good. This is not a denial of "the goodness of God," but a refutation of God by man. *In the catastrophic events (earthquakes, eruptions, tidal waves, and storms), nature itself seems to deny "the goodness of God." Comment on this anomaly.*

Question 4. Today there is little reverence for the dignity of human beings, life, nature, and the world in which we live. *If you accept that you have a part in the preservation of all that is good, what will you do about it—now—in this moment, in this lifetime?*

"I bow my knees unto the Father, ... That he would grant you, according to the riches of his glory, to be strengthened with might by his Spirit in the inner man."
—Ephesians 3:14,16

"STIMULATORS TO ACTION"–

Inspiration is a gift from God–
Aspiration is the desire we have to do
With that which has been given.
Accomplishment
comes only because
We have done something with that
Which God has given!

Inspiration, aspiration, and dedication assure that: *"Every good gift and every perfect gift is from above, and cometh down from the Father of lights, with whom is no variableness, neither shadow of turning." –James 1:17*

The Law of Cause and Effect

Within a short time after being blessed with being on this earth, most mature and reasonable adults realize that neither they nor others are self-contained or sufficient unto themselves. Survival, in a physical sense, demands constant increment of resources beyond one's individual energy and skill. Reliance on the abilities of others to produce that which sustains is essential.

OUR RELIANCE ON OTHERS

For a great portion of our lives we are dependent on the knowledge and wisdom of others who preceded. Without others' learning, preserved for those yet unborn, how difficult the way would be! There is no inherent knowledge of ourselves other than a few instinctive qualities. Without others, what a paucity indeed! Without an interlacing of man and man and mind and mind we would be nescient, unenlightened, uninstructed, unlettered, unwitting, unaware and ignorant. And yet we reject the linkages giving freedom and bind ourselves by that which we think frees us. We are *"rebels without a cause."*

The causes for most of the things we do lie within ourselves. The causes of what we can become lie beyond us. We may survive, but we cannot really live sufficient unto ourselves. We are of a reluctant consciousness—without a cause—we rebel.

Let us examine why men such as Thomas Paine, Jesus Christ, and many others were not trapped within the narrow confines of self-interest, but chose, rather, to represent the cause beyond the self. Was their stand rebellion or was it recognition that what they stood for extended, augmented, and gave increase to more than just themselves? They stood for something! Their cause was just: and they had reason to rebel.

You need not stand for hedonistic ideology or believe in altruistic verbiage. You must stand for something for yourself. Admit to it or not, reject it or accept it—this must include others, and something more than you and they. *Some call it "God."*

YOUR ASSIGNMENT FOR THIS WEEK

Whenever we are asked to change our thinking, attitudes or concepts, we are challenged. We are ready to employ measures of resistance, for we did not develop into what we are overnight. Do not rebel without a cause. The effect may not be what you would wish.

Release completely all that experience has told you about yourself, your God, and your fellow man. Be receptive to a new experience and a deeper understanding. Rebel in the sense that beyond convention there are doctrines, reasons and motives for action other than discussion and debate. Let your cause be meaningful: seek that meaning in all things, persons, times, and places.

Decide, beginning this moment, to do something specifically for someone for whom you would do nothing. Decide to give meaning where meaning is but a word. Give, and give of yourself. With a willingness to accept what good may return, expect nothing in return.

Relax in the knowledge that you and others and God are one. While this may sound like idle chatter that is difficult to know, it can be known.

And now, for more than a moment, go for a walk—alone. Walk upon a street or in the wood, or pause beside a stream: a stream of running water, or the stream of consciousness of God and fellow man. But walk, and walk alone.

What will you learn? *One question. One answer. One source. One with the other.* Write down what you do feel.

MAKE THIS—
YOUR DAILY AFFIRMATION FOR THE WEEK:
"I use the word "God" this day and henceforth, to represent that source of all I have, of all I need, in each experience I will seek that which is of God!!"

Your basis of reality in daily living

How easily we proclaim that God is present everywhere, all-knowing, and all-powerful! Then we look and do not find that which we have proclaimed. But have we looked? We seek the presence of God and do not find the God we seek. If only He could tell us where He is in this life! Thus we program God and our good in far and distant future—in a time beyond the here and now. We limit God and do not listen nor perceive that He is in the faintest scent and sound and is the power and presence in all that we see, hear, do and are.

"This day I act and think in a different way. I perceive the presence of God in all things. The words I use are representations of what I feel, think, and know. I use the word "God" today and henceforth to represent that source of all I have, all I need, and all I know. But even more, I use the word "God" to represent all those with whom I come in contact. *In each experience I will seek that which is of God."*

An important consideration—

In most cases one is much the same after reading a book as when one started. There is little change. The necessary inner change can only be made through contemplation, self-discipline and involvement. The material and the questions presented in this book require involvement and offer opportunity for the necessary change. As you proceed from week to week, participating in the discipline, your life, your affairs and you yourself will change.

Your self-development questions

Question 1. Every century has produced men and women who stood for something—who were individuals of conscience. Each "rebelled" for a cause of mind or spirit, or the humanistic concept. Well remembered are those who bore these names: *Christ, Ramakrishna, Channing, Emerson, John Dewey, Holmes, Brandeis, Thorstein Veblen, Ruskin, Thoreau, Ida Tarbell, Stephen Crane, Jane Addams, Charles Kingsley.* The list, though long, is not infinite. These persons of intellect and conscience each sought to shape and determine life to a better degree for others. They were "rebels with a cause." *In this day and age many rebel against many things—within their minds. What cause of conscience could you give yourself to which would make this world better than it is?*

Question 2. Demosthenes, in his oration, *"Measures to Resist Philip,"* declared, *"It is impossible, . . . to have a high and noble spirit while you are engaged in petty and mean employment; whatever be the pursuits of men, their character must be similar."* These are more than simple statements of truth; they are hard, cold facts. *Would you know God? Would you have a better life? What will you do to make it better for all men?*

Question 3. Life is legitimate drama. All else is but acting of a play obscuring the individual while making reality seem unreal. While we can receive vicarious satisfaction through the antics, effort, enterprise, and ability of those who dramatically and delightfully entertain us, there comes a time we must face reality and stop looking at life as an "event upon a stage." *Formulate a rule of greater fulfillment.*

Question 4. Objective criticism is valid and valuable thought projected toward and concerning something in need of change. Those of us who recognize what is wrong, i.e., in need of change, are in the best position to do something about what should be changed or improved, rather than merely find fault with it. *Give thought to one thing in your life, your association, your environment, your circumstances, or your condition that is in need of change. What will you do to change this?*

"Produce your cause, saith the Lord; bring forth your strong reasons." —Isaiah 41:21

"STIMULATORS TO ACTION"–

What would you do?
Give thought to that which you would do.
Now give added thought to how and dwell upon
this night and day.
And as you think, and think, and think,
and dream, and dream, and dream, and pray—
You will find—there is a way!
What would you do?

**The importance of the
broad view**

As we look at the world of nature around us, we see everything traveling in one direction—toward expression and fulfillment. A river meanders, but always toward a larger body of water. The tree grows from seed to root, fiber, bark, branches, and leaves—to an expression of its total self. The river grows, widens, expands and serves a purpose as it moves along its natural course. As it joins with other streams it becomes more than a thing of beauty and a meandering stream. It supports the commerce of a world filled with men: it feeds and nourishes, sustains, and gives pleasure to those who love the rivers, lakes, and seas.

The tree grows from a tiny seed to a sturdy oak. It fulfills its purpose of holding the soil and preventing erosion and flood. As it absorbs minerals and nutrients from the soil, it grows sturdy and strong. As it breathes in light and warmth from the sun, it gives in return oxygen to sustain the world around it. But it does not stop there, nor does it stop with giving shelter and shade and being a thing of beauty. It provides houses, homes, walls, doors, floors, tables and numerous other things.

Both the river and the tree—and all of nature—follow a pattern of development—expression, expansion, and giving—and a course natural to this development—*unless interfered with by man. And man not only does not find his own fulfillment—he disrupts the balance of nature around him.*

As we look at the world of nature around us, we can see that everything *is* traveling in one direction: toward fulfillment and expression. Man seems to be the only aspect of life that becomes other than what he was meant to be. Even the common rock is a rock. The blade of grass, the weed, the bush, the shrub and the plant do not stop short of what they were meant to be. We may say, "A river and a tree are without choice. Therefore each must follow the course set before it." We can also say, "Man is a volitional being and can choose what course he will follow, what direction he will take, and what he will be." For many it would seem wise to ask, "Why have they chosen the direction they have, and become what they have? Especially if they have choice?" Perhaps we have chosen the wrong path, channel or direction through error. Perhaps we became less than we might have been because we just didn't know at a particular time just what to do. What can we do to direct our life with meaning, and with a direction that is constant?

If a river ceases to flow, move, expand and serve a purpose beyond itself, the water stagnates. If a tree ceases to extend its roots, if it ceases to draw substance from the earth upon which it stands, and ceases to grow and give—it dies. If you and I, as men, cease to have directed goals and purposes that will give meaning to others as well as to ourselves we will stagnate, wither, and die. Perhaps this is not true in the same sense as it is for the river and the tree, but most certainly our lives will lack much that will make them rich and abundant. Just exactly *how* can we make our lives rich and abundant? There lies before us, at any given time, a choice. If we don't like things the way they are, or if we would improve our lives, conditions and circumstances, we can decide to do something about these things. What can we do? How do you start your day? With a desire to remain in bed? With exercise? Or with a patterned habit, continuing on as before, without much thought to what the day will bring?

Each day we channel and chart our course. We can make the decision to determine that "This day is mine!" Or we can give no thought to it, with the result, "I'll take what comes." In the latter case we have no reason for complaint, and not much more for living.

Rather than taking what comes, we can make what comes. We do this by setting aside something very human—"human consciousness"—our awareness of things as they appear to be, and determining direction by and through the "Christ consciousness" or "creative consciousness." This places a demand on us. We start out with a word, prayer, aspiration, hope or inspiration. And then we nourish it, give thought to it, channel it, and direct it until it evolves into a greater expression which sustains, supports, and gives meaning, life, purpose to others besides ourselves.

Different levels of development

Life most certainly exists on different levels of development. The vegetative level lacks consciousness. I'm not sure that animals are as aware as are we of the many different aspects of life, but I am certain that animal life has an awareness greater than the credit we ascribe to it. However, you and I, as men, have developed to a point where we can choose to move about the face of this earth, where no rock, ridge or mountain gorge stands in our way. We can carve and create or corrupt and destroy our world, our fellow man and our selves. We can take a thought, idea or concept, and through discipline, nurture it into the sound of music, a book of inspiration, or a living temple representative of him whom we called Christ. We can take a dream, give it roots and help it grow. This dream will receive its nourishment from channeled direction, or wither and die from neglect. We can take our life and follow the direction, pattern or channel cut deep and wide by the life of a man who lived long ago and far away. We can choose which channel our consciousness will take. But we cannot live and grow and have and give meaning—and be what too many, for too long, have been—"a river of two streams."

**How a woman succeeded in
being accepted by others**

*"I don't relate to people. I don't like them. And I would thank
you to keep your lousy thoughts to yourself."* My heart went out
to this woman who rejected the world—while all the while
reaching out, desperately seeking and needing the very thing of
which she said she wanted no part.

How does one help one who refuses help? With this question
uppermost in my mind, I quietly stepped aside, saying, "There are
times I don't relate to people. There are times I don't like them.
And there are times when I would thank them to keep their lousy
thoughts to themselves. So, really, we are not so very different
from each other, are we?" She looked at me and said, "You are
still sharing your lousy thoughts with me, aren't you?" "Yep! Yes
ma'am! You are right. And I will do my darnedest to keep my
mouth shut and mind my own business."

We sat opposite each other for perhaps an hour before she
finally blurted out, "Why in the devil don't you say something?
You got a mouth ain't you?" I look at her, smiled, and said not a
word. Returning my look, she started to laugh. "I don't really
dislike people. I do want to relate to them. I want so desperately
to relate to people and to have them like me and accept me. And I
do want you to tell me what to do—please, please—please tell me
what to do so that people will like me and so that I won't be so
lonely." Without saying a word, I reached out my hand and drew
her close, putting my arm around her shoulder. "Now why did
you do that? You up to something? Are you?" How like "the seed
on barren ground"! She would have friends, she would know
meaning, and whatever she "planted" took root on barren and
fallow ground.

"I put my arm around you because that is exactly what you
needed. And yes, I am up to something." I then asked her a
question: "What is it you would have in your life? Friends? Then
you must be a friend. Is it happiness instead of loneliness at whose
table you would sup? Then think a kind and loving thought—and
even more—share this thought with another, for the world is filled
with people seeking just what you and I are seeking—and most of

them seek in vain because they do not know that one cannot receive without giving. What is it you would have? Prosperity? Peace of mind? Abundance? There is a principle, a rule, a law, a doctrine which must be followed. And it works exactly the same for every man and woman on the face of this earth." She started to listen. "What is the rule? How do I do what I must do?" Sharing a philosophy that has determined my own life, this woman gradually found in life, circumstances and the events of her life far more than she had ever dreamed. (She now operates a school based on what she discovered. Let's call it "Friendship!")

How to Regulate the Streams of Consciousness Within Ourselves

At this moment join with me in an observation. In your mind conceive of yourself many miles above the earth. Below, transmitted from distant earth, a far different panorama lies before you. Vast, sweeping fields and plains reach out and blend with towering mountains. Clouds that viewed with uplifted eyes billowed and formed fantastic shapes now appear mere wisps of gray and white. But other things have changed as well. That solitary river bares the blending veins of other, smaller rivers, streams, and trickles—coming together to make a mighty river. We can see, perhaps for the first time, what we have always known: without each added stream, our river would not exist. And in deeper contemplation, logic tells us, "reverse the flow of water into a channel of many streams—and each no longer exists."

A river of two streams

We are, each of us, a river of two streams: alert or dull, kind or cruel, conscious or unconscious, doing and succeeding, or striving, struggling, and failing. We are spiritual or without spirit. Reach out to that subtle, silent, unseen force which we call *"He,"* let it join with that which we are: "man." If we allow it to encompass and become one with us, we have a word spelled *"h—U—man—e."* The connotations are all that one could seek: *regard for others, kindness, compassion, benevolence, refined knowledge, elevation, spirituality.*

We are a river of two streams—two streams of consciousness: one that lifts and sustains, or one that draws, drains and depletes us of that which we were meant to be.

YOUR ASSIGNMENT FOR THIS WEEK

Through the refinement and simplicity of a sincere desire, we channel and choose our stream of consciousness.

Gravitation holds us to this planet without any effort on our part. Spirit continually draws us to it in untold ways. We break loose by a constant, concerted effort to attract ourselves to that which seems to be not of the spirit.

Now: Leave reason, question and complaint aside. Within your mind create the image that *you are a channel*. View all that is about you in a new perspective: know that all and everything has good in it. Envisage all that is good in whatever you look upon as a channel flowing toward and into you. Do not for a moment allow anything except that you *are* receiving from each tiny stream you call an incident, growing stronger from an ever-flowing source from all directions. And know that as you grow, you give and give and give—for you have life-sustaining resources as you have received them.

Be as the river could it talk, converse, and know: "Without all that flows to me, I would not be." Be as the river, a mighty source, both giving and receiving.

At this time, reread all that has been given in this lesson. Then quietly contemplate all that issues forth toward you.

"A man shall be . . . as rivers of water in a dry place." —Isaiah 32:2

MAKE THIS—

YOUR DAILY AFFIRMATION FOR THE WEEK:

"As water flowing to the sea effortlessly follows the course of least resistance, I now select and choose the path reducing effort and resistance: faith in God, in myself and in my fellow man. There is but one way to do this—with every thought. Make this thought more than words alone—make it action!"

**Your basis of reality
in daily living**

All of us have faith in something. What we have faith in determines that which is good or less than good in our life. Do you accept this? Or do you say, "I have faith—but my life has not been productive of that which I have sought." If these words are the silent issue of your heart and the visible issue of your affairs, consider this: Did you not believe in, have faith in and have interest in what you succeeded in? If you are old before your time, do you not believe in age? If you are healthy and happy, and your life is meaningful—have you not placed your faith in this?

"As water flowing to the sea effortlessly follows the course of least resistance, I now select and choose the path reducing effort and resistance: faith in God, in myself and in my fellow man. There is but one way to do this—with every thought. Make this thought more than words alone—make it action!"

A constructive reflection—

As a man's religion is not the church of his choice or the creed he proclaims, his life is not what he thinks or hopes or aspires to, but the doctrine by which he lives—the discipline determining his life.

Your self-development questions

Question 1. Interplanetary travel requires the most precise scientific knowledge. Nothing like this kind of knowledge is needed to journey to the farthest reaches of the spirit. *But what is necessary to enter the realm of Spirit?*

Question 2. The most tragic irony of every life is that each individual has within his reach what will enable him to reach beyond any limitation—if he will but use it. No man is without moments of spiritual awareness, no matter how rare. Somewhere on this journey through life he is acutely aware of the power and potential that is his, if he will respond to more than the individual self. But he seems to want to play the fool. *If you would be more creative and cease cutting channels through the hardest of rock, what would you do to become that single flowing stream of elevated consciousness?*

Question 3. In every life there comes a time for appraisal. To all there must be more than a moment when the individual asks himself, "Where am I going and how do I get there?" There is not a moment of our lives when we are not on a road leading us toward what we would have—or away from it. We are always at a fork in the road, reaching a river of two streams—and traveling one or the other. *How can we always proceed so that we make the right choice, without error or regret?*

Question 4. Wherever we travel in this life, on this earth, in consciousness, or in our dreams, hopes, fantasies, fears, frustrations, or aspirations, we can never quite go back to where we were. We will either move ahead, grow, develop, and expand—and thus express—or we will regress. *Both discipline and spirit will help us on our way. What one other essential is necessary to growth in any way?*

"When the desire cometh, it is a tree of life." —Proverbs 13:12

How Nancy overcame her crushing humiliations

A year in a psychiatric hospital, shock treatment, drugs, sleeping pills, a broken marriage, jail, a suicide attempt—hardly the pattern for a successful and productive life. At most, complete and utter failure; at least, prostituted potential. This young woman in her twenties had run the gamut of despair, heartbreak, failure and frustration.

There was little doubt in my mind that Nancy was striving to find meaning in her life, communicate with others, and establish a dialogue with life, but her approach was all wrong. Drawing her out, I observed that she used people not really knowing that this was what she was doing. In her desperate attempt to have others accept her, she experienced all the hell and agony that she sought to avoid. In getting to know her, I thought of a chapter of a manuscript I was then writing, "How rare it is that we utilize the tremendous potential we have. And how often we are little more than a 'Shadow of the Self.' "

To me, Nancy was a challenge—and a wonderful opportunity. How does it feel to be an instrument in the remaking of a life? To see a young woman bent on self-destruction come back from the brink of disaster? I've been asked this question many times. The answer is not a simple one. The feeling is good—and we have all experienced it in some way or another in relation to our fellow man.

A program of definite disciplines was set before this young woman. Equally important—she followed the disciplines or programs. Within two weeks Nancy was free from sleeping pills and tranquilizers. Today this young woman is holding down a responsible position in a leading company.

"STIMULATORS TO ACTION"—

Open the door which closets your clothes.
Neatly arranged—or disarray?
If a mixed-up muddle— Begin!
Straighten out what is nearest to you—day by day.
Now,
Open wide the door encompassing
What is within your mind.
As with your closet and your clothes—order—arrange—
and with some things dispose. Each time—first thing of each
and every day—a reminder of the order necessary
to stimulated action.
Do it now: it will pay!

How to Deal with the
Shadow of the Real Self

You and I know that we are more than the contemplated thought—the unfulfilled dream. Every seed completely expresses the fullness from within its being. The acorn grows to oak; the raindrop to a river or stream—each the fullness of itself and of time and place. *Man alone remains a shadow of the self.* Yet he has within himself all he needs for fulfillment, as does that which he considers less than self. And that which he considers less than himself expresses fullness of purpose and intent. *He alone remains shadow instead of substance.*

Man knows that he has a mind, intellect and spirit. He looks upon the lowest form of life and observes that nature gives it no choice. Would that he would look beyond the choice and know that all that is less then himself becomes all that it was meant to be! He alone can be more than man by the same urge that gives no choice to seed and weed and tree. They cannot say "I will not grow, develop, and be that which I was meant to be." Given the slightest opportunity—moisture, light, air—each seed will seek, strive and grow.

We pass up countless opportunities, not because we have the choice, but because we make no choice. And because we make no choice, we remain but a shadow of the self.

Every man possesses the gentle spirit of justification of the silent dream—of the tangibility of substance rather than the mistlike quality of a dissolute shadow. We ask: why? We have been given choice. Our heartfelt desire must be, in knowing truth, to know the meaning of the truth of choice. We are not above all else and *"A little lower than the angels"* for shallow reasons.

"Meditate upon these things;
Give thyself wholly to them." —I Timothy 4:15

YOUR ASSIGNMENT FOR THIS WEEK

We have been given choice. Ask "Why?" and prayerfully seek the answer.

In your own manner and by your own choosing, select the way of seeking to know the "why?"

On a separate sheet, set out the answers to the following:

My spiritual discipline for this coming week:

What would I like to be—over and above what I have been?

I aspire to:

The means of fulfillment are what I must do:

By freedom of will, you and I exercise independence of the vagaries of our minds. We cannot determine one thing and have another. We can, if we would, by the soothing suasion of immortal truth, know our eternal worth.

"There is a spirit in man: and the inspiration of the Almighty giveth them understanding." —Job 32:8

MAKE THIS—

YOUR DAILY AFFIRMATION FOR THE WEEK:

I have free will. I exercise wisdom in the freedom of this will. I hold to lofty thoughts and inspiration becomes aspiration—I achieve what I seek."

Your basis of reality
in daily living

On rare occasions something creates a compelling desire, constraining us to more than witness the character of life. We are obliged and compensated. A sudden vision or an intense longing precipitates inquiry into understanding. We plunge headlong—body, mind, soul, spirit, and affairs—into our endeavor for spiritual illumination: we seek and find. No longer are we a "Shadow of the Self," but part and parcel of all that is and one with God. "I" witness the eternal flux and change and know my part. I stand beside the stream of life and know I am that current—that moving course of concept, idea, fruition, event, opinion, the evil inflicted, and the good bestowed. I am the life-blood of twist and turn, blasphemy or blessing. I am the shadow or the self.

"I have free will. I exercise wisdom in the freedom of this will. I hold to lofty thoughts and inspiration becomes aspiration—I achieve what I seek."

A point to ponder—

The unity of man and God is not a matter of you and a distant spirit. It is a purpose and principle of present participation.

Your self development questions

Question 1. In the realm of philosophy, an individual is involved and evolves by the process and power of thought. In the domain of religion, the individual can (but rarely does) authenticate the power of spirit. Philosophy is assumed to be an authority of the mind; religion, the assuasive authority of spirit. Among the definitions of "authority," is: "an accepted source of information." Emerson, who authenticated both philosophy and religion, makes two statements—one clear, and one of consideration and question. *1. "... the soul that ascends to worship the great God is plain and true; dwells in the hour that now is, in the earnest experience of the common day—by reason of the present movement and the mere trifle having become porous to thought and ... of the sea of light ..." 2. "The faith that stands on authority measures the decline of religion—the withdrawal of the soul."* Consideration: *In the light of his first statement, what is the meaning of the second?*

Question 2. While it is impossible to define religion in a sentence due to its diverse aspects which affect human existence at different times and places, we can say that the ultimate aim of realization is harmony between God and man—the aspiring individual and the principle of integration. *We know what we ask of religion. What does religion demand of us?*

Question 3. The evolution of the world or the individual involves a continual creative process. In nature, what is created has purpose and function. *Why is it so often that man, genuinely seeking to "evolve," appears at variance with himself, nature, God, and his fellow man?*

Question 4. Each man can be a channel of spiritual power to those around him. *Specify ways in which you will be this channel for each day of the coming week on a separate sheet. Carry this sheet with you to remind yourself of your progress.*

> **"There is neither Jew nor Greek, there is neither bond nor free, there is neither male nor female: for ye are all one in Christ Jesus."**
> **—Galatians 3:28**

"STIMULATORS TO ACTION"—

An idea, a desire, a hope, a dream,
An aspiration—pursued.
You have many ideas.
Every once in a while a profound, workable, meaningful idea
will come to you—pursue it! Extract from it
all it contains. This becomes the
Stimulus for an ever increasing abundance of worthy ideas
and workable ideals.
Action is the word!
Pursue your dream
and your dream will overtake you
in fulfillment.
"Seek . . . and pursue . . . " —Psalm 34:14

WEEKLY PROGRAM
NUMBER

6

How to Give the Devil His Due

A note of importance: *This series of exercises and points to ponder are not only for those new to the practice of spiritual achievement but also for those who are far along the way.*

A reminder: *In a place of quiet, alone, or with a kindred spirit, quietly contemplate that which precedes the assignment itself.*

Remember, *you are free to observe and apply spiritual disciplines. You will be rewarded for the effort. The consequences of ignoring what can be done will not pass unnoticed.*

When we probe to the depth of most individuals, we apprehend that "depth" to be diluted by disorder and lack of discipline. Conceding that the world is of our mind and of our making, we can easily comprehend the importance of order and discipline in effecting accomplishment. Disorder results in "the Devil to Pay!" To you the "Devil" may be the "hell you raise." I would prefer to hope that it is the result of misdirected but honest effort. The result is the same—we lose. I say "we lose" instead of "you lose" intentionally, for when anyone neither gives nor receives his best, we cannot honestly say, "He is the only loser!"

It would be possible to compose volumes indicting those who fail to achieve any desired end, solely because of nonobservance of the good. So there is hell to pay—and the Devil extracts his ducat.

To truly achieve the potential within his grasp, all one has to do is to determine to hold to a loftier view, confine complaints to periods of unconsciousness, release all that hints of less than good, positive, constructive consideration, and regard oneself as the most

47

fortunate person in the world. The Devil will have received his due
in the form of barren and fallow reverie.

If the Devil (unproductive thought) has a tight hold on you,
consider: *How sweet a breath of air is to a drowning man. How
valuable a drink of water is to one with thirst. How blessed a
morsel of food to one who is hungry, or companion to him who
has known loneliness.*

The only way we beat the Devil at his own game is to not give
in to self-destructive thought; to hold to that which we would
have, rather than to that which we would be rid of; to give thanks
for the myriad blessings we have and may have minimized through
thoughtless unconcern. *Example:* Give thanks for the silence when
you are alone. Hold a positive thought!

"Let us go on unto perfection." —Hebrews 6:1

YOUR ASSIGNMENT FOR THIS WEEK

**"Now I know in part; but then shall I know even as also I am
known." —I Corinthians 13:12**

Take a pad and pencil. Write down at least a dozen things you
know are not good.

Now: Direct your mind to discovering what is good in each
object, situation, circumstance or person.

Finally: Perceive what YOU can do to make better what you
know is not good. Write these perceptions down. Carry them with
you and read at least a dozen times this week. And as you do, a
new intent and purpose will possess you, carrying you to unaccus-
tomed discoveries of the world in which you are now beginning to
live.

And—

**"Instead of the thorn shall come up the fir tree, and instead of the brier
shall come up the myrtle tree." —Isaiah 55:13**

and then—

"Thou shalt see greater things than these." —John 1:50

The conscious evolution of each of us lies deep within the
words we use, and the thoughts we have. The meanings we give to

thoughts and words become deeds. The only Devil we ever know is a truth unvalued; an opportunity ignored; a challenge untried; and a vision narrowed to where we stand. From any other view it is impossible to acknowledge that which we would know.

"Then shall we know, if we follow on to know the Lord,"*
—Hosea 6:3

MAKE THIS—

YOUR DAILY AFFIRMATION FOR THE WEEK:

"Every thought that is unproductive I erase from my mind and affairs—now. In its stead, I seek and search—in every condition, circumstance, and person—only that which is good, uplifting, and of benefit to them and to myself."

Your basis of reality in daily living

The expression, "Give the Devil his due" is not an unfamiliar one. What is the Devil? To some the Devil is an entity residing in a stronghold called Hell. He is called many names: Satan, Lucifer, Belial, the Evil One, the Prince of Darkness, the Adversary—but they all suggest that which keeps us from our highest expression of good. To give the Devil his due it becomes our responsibility to allow absolutely nothing to keep our highest good from being manifested.

Give the Devil his due! Unproductive thoughts, unrewarding effort and denigrating conditions return nothing to you: give nothing to them. Most certainly a man is "worthy of his hire." If a man was unproductive we would not pay him. If he not only was unproductive, but took from us worthy effort, returning discouragement, disillusionment, and failure, we would soon be well rid of him. *Give the Devil his due!*

A helpful supporting affirmation

"Every thought that is unproductive I erase from my mind and affairs—now. In its stead, I seek and search—in every condition,

---

*The law of your own being.

circumstance, and person—only that which is good, uplifting, and of benefit to them and to myself."

Reflect—Christianity, theology, religion, the reading of a book, knowing what to do—none of these will change you or your life. *The disciplines you observe will.*

Your self-development questions

Question 1. The term "metaphysics" is one that is used more commonly each day. In turning to the dictionary, we find the definition inadequate. There seems to be a profusion of meanings. *What does "metaphysics" imply to you?*

Question 2. From the Apocrypha (scripture not incorporated in our Bible) we know that in wealth one knows not his friends, and in poverty and affliction one is certain of his enemies. It would appear that it indeed would be difficult to *know* our friends during affluence. The second statement requires no comment. *Question: How could one with wealth be certain of YOUR integrity? How would your answer appear different from that of a sharp "con artist" whose stock in trade is making others aware of his sincerity and integrity?*

Question 3. "Sunday Religion" is for "someday" people. Religion is an extension of *what* you are—NOT what you are reaching for. A religion for every moment is a constant declaration of spiritual principles by which you live and which others can experience. *What insights have you incorporated, or can you blend into your life from the last three times you have heard a sermon?* This may require considerable reflection.

Question 4. The most important period of your life is the present. However your past thinking has brought you to this particular state of mind and condition of life. In the future, much that you experience will be directly attributable to your evolving consciousness—your "frame of reference"—how you think now and in the time that is yet to be. *What image do you hold for yourself one year from now? Five years from now? Ten years from now? If you don't have one, it is wisdom to determine a goal. DETERMINE A GOAL! NOW!*

"I have set the Lord [divine consciousness; inner creative power; the law of my own being] always before me." —Psalm 16:8

"STIMULATORS TO ACTION"–

Possibly one of the greatest "stimulators to action"
is the power of a creative mind. Should you
ask what relationship there is between a creative
mind and action, the answer would be: the ability to
see beyond the visible. A more explicit answer would
be: What one can conceive in the mind, one can achieve!
Retention of an image which others may not perceive is
a stimulant to action. How does one express creative
imagery? Contemplate a block of wood.
To what uses can it be put?
It may become sculpture, match sticks, paper,
toothpicks, pencils, a paper weight, or a steppingstone.
Contemplate the familiar. Within it there is a "stimulator
to action"!

7

The Power of Concentration
on Meditation and The Silence

"It is not thinking that counts but unfoldment." —Thomas L. Masson

"Bread does not support life. If it did, one could put food into the body of a dead man, lay him out in the sun, and expect him to come to life." —Paramahansa Yogananda

Nor is it thought alone, nor desire, nor the fact that we would know God that gives us knowledge of God. In all forms of life there is a subtle unseen energy supporting, sustaining, motivating and moving—without which there is no life.

As the physical body requires food, water, and air, the energizing force from which we gain life—and through which we evolve spiritually—requires our attention for the development of ideas and understanding. Unfortunately, we too often give our attention only to that which interests us. Thus we experience pain or pleasure. To the degree of our concentration, *we experience.* If we would experience what is good and of God, we must concentrate on it. It is not the momentary thought that brings unfolding, but the idea or the desire that is sustained. As we concentrate upon what gives life, that life is concentrated in us and expressed through us.

The entire history of man is one of spiritual impoverishment. He thinks of words and not of ways, means and purpose. He would succeed by exploitation and effort of the mind. He would succeed for himself—but he fails instead. He can succeed by definitive effort and purpose, and placing himself and his affairs

52

with that which unfolds. Admit it or not, most of us are interested in the reward rather than the discipline, in the results rather than the effort. The discipline is a necessity if we are not to be divested of the meaning.

Definition and discipline:

Concentration is the ability to direct and channel the mind on thoughts of your selection.

Meditation is concentration to *know* God.

The Silence *is knowing communication with God. (Knowing God can be experienced under all circumstances, including periods of stillness or the Silence).*

YOUR ASSIGNMENT FOR THIS WEEK

Assume a comfortable position, back straight, hands resting in lap, palms upward. Expell breath rapidly to the mental count of three. Make no effort to inhale. Rather, allow the breath to return and flow gently and naturally. Repeat this exercise for a period of three to five minutes.

Now: Exhale deeply. If able, hold to the count of 20 before inhaling. Inhale. Hold to the count of 20, or less, if this is difficult at first. Do this for approximately five minutes. *Then release* all thought except *"Calm,"* picturing in your mind a scene that is calm, peaceful, and serene.

For at least thirty minutes daily, continue this exercise. During this time silently affirm: *"Calm, peace, serenity."*

An ever-increasing sense of peace and an inner awareness that your affairs—inner and outer—are changing for the better, will determine your progress.

During this coming week make note of the changes you observe within yourself and your affairs. Note them on a separate sheet of paper.

"Apply thine heart unto instruction, and thine ears to the words of knowledge." —Proverbs 23:12

MAKE THIS—

YOUR DAILY AFFIRMATION FOR THE WEEK:

"I concern myself only with that which will elevate my consciousness
and direct my life toward the understanding of myself and my fellow
man, and I seek awareness of God in all things."

Your basis of reality
in daily living

Fundamental to the understanding of any truth is that I envision
beyond part of that which I would comprehend. To know the
whole, I cannot settle for a portion. Accepting less than the
totality of truth obscures the truth, takes us no farther than our
starting point, and always leaves us with a "cloud of unknowing"—
a mist beyond which intellect alone will not traverse.

Acquainting ourselves with superficialities leaves only superficialities. As in algebra we accept the hypothesis that X equals an
unknown quantity, we must embrace that there is more to
everything than a cursory examination reveals. Postulate beyond
appearance. The depths are profound. Accept this: All thought
can lead to God *when I concern myself only with that which will
elevate my consciousness and direct my life toward the understanding of myself and my fellow man, and seek awareness of God
in all things.*

An important consideration—What really counts is not the
dream of distant accomplishment nor deeply held hope, but that
which we do beyond the dream which justifies hope.

Your self-development questions

Question 1. The power of the mind has fantastic potential. It is
this potential that is referred to when we are counseled to "Know
Thyself." But it is always the unknown, not the known, that we
must seek to know. How can this be?

Question 2. Christians are inclined to believe that an ascending
spiritual consciousness will result in a lessening of suffering for the

individual. *Jesus Christ was the most noble example of an "evolved" consciousness. He suffered during His short life and died an ignoble death in agony. How do we resolve these apparent inconsistencies?*

Question 3. First stated by Lao Tse, propounded by Zen, and dimly perceived by all who truly seek to "know" beyond the self, the idea that "I do not know; therefore I possess all the knowledge there is," is part of every religion. *How would you explain this unalterable truth?*

Question 4. The "spiritual life" has been relegated to Sunday mornings and to times of hardship or profound experience. *Other than going to church every Sunday morning, reading the scriptures, and being good, what can, should, and must we do to grow spiritually? And what is spiritual growth?*

> "Meditate upon these things; give thyself wholly to them; that thy profiting may appear to all." —I Timothy 4:15

How a convict at the bottom of the heap helped himself to success

Against overwhelming odds, one can prove the power of the application of a workable, provable, demonstrable principle. I first met "Stratton" in a maximum security prison. Rounding the corner of a corridor, there he stood—physically, one of the biggest human beings I have ever seen.

After getting to know this man, I learned there were other "big" things about him—his "time," for one. He was serving what would be to most a lifetime for attempted kidnapping and attempted murder: "a hard rap," as he put it. Over the period of three years of my association with him I saw an embittered and violent man rise to the occasion and put into practice the psychology of mind dynamics, against overwhelming odds, by using his dynamic but long-dormant mind.

There are many thrilling incidents in life. One of the great rewards of my life is to recall what happened to this "long-term" con. After I left the prison ministry I had little contact with this man for the next several years. Then one day a letter arrived, telling me of how, although everything was against his getting out, except "for you, and the power you conveyed to me that lies within my own mind to determine my own life and destiny. Most certainly through God—but by God—It's up to the man himself to believe, and apply, and *prove!*"

Stratton now operates a modest but successful business, and lectures to groups of prison and state officials and businessmen about practical ways in which men and women can help themselves.

"STIMULATORS TO ACTION"–

Determine to have the courage to be yourself.
The first requisite is that you have a good opinion
of yourself and your potential for expressive creativity—
giving little thought to the impression you are going to make
on others—
they are more concerned with the impression they are
going to make on you.
If you believe in something, anything, have the courage to pursue
Pursuing what you really believe in is the ground spring,
the stimulus that motivates further action.

HOW TO RAISE THE MISTS IN DAILY LIVING

For as long as man has been on this earth, other men have been here with him. Yet as long as he has been here, he has remained *a stranger to himself.* He does not know himself for what he is, or others for what they can be. No one really understands *his* hopes and fears or comprehends *his* frustrations. *He does not know that black or white or brown or yellow or red or young or old—the man who walks a different path walks side by side with him.*

He seeks, and others seek. But the search is desperate for neither knows what is being sought nor how to seek it. He knows only endless words and phrases. "I would know God. I would have peace. I would the world would be a better place for you and me." *And any attempt by Nature and by that rare, enlightened One to point the way, bring him back to his point of no departure. He is,* as it were, betrothed to a mist obscuring vision—wedded to the raucous sound of a thousand intents and one continuous frustration. He cannot hear the sound of the silence of his own soul, or the heartbeat within the breast of everything in this vast universe. He cannot see—he does not hear—*he will not listen—to the silent sound of God!* His mind, his heart, and the Good Book tell him, "Be still and know that I am God!" But the simplicity of the admonition refutes the truth; he will not try it. Sometimes he will, for a moment, listen and nod his head and say, "I agree," and continue as he has for the last ten or twenty years. He himself is the "mist" before his eyes. By the process of "self-enclosure" he narrows the confines of the world in which he would live. He changes nothing by agreement or assent. By *action* he will transform himself and the world in which he exists. In using the term "he," I am really talking about "we." At times we dimly perceive that the "mist of illusion" concealing all that elevates the consciousness can be raised. If we would dispel the mist, we must relate. We must relate, for without relationships there is no meaning. The relationship of a man and a woman create a family. The relating of families creates communities. Communities form cities, states and nations. And the people of a nation are a society in which we are not independent but interdependent. Our mind tells us, "I am a soul with choice and I can choose as I will." Your mind is right. But a question comes to mind: "Why choose less than the best? Why live in the half-shadow of life when life can lift all that obscures, darkens, and deepens meaning into something less than meaning?"

It's impossible to know all of God, each of our fellow man, and everything that has existed or will exist. But we can know that all and everything *is* God. And if we can accept without knowing—we will know, accept, embrace and relate to *all* and *each* and *everything*.

I would depart from the stand (a poor one at that) that a Supreme Being exists—looking down on you and me, showing any greater concern for us than we do for it. This is the first myth I would dispense with. *When we cease praying to a God of our own creation, we may be able to effectively relate to the God of all creation.* God is not something we are reaching for but something we are: *that* which is deep within the heart of man and stone and every drop of rain, every seed, impulse and thought. That God we would know *is* the quality and essence of every dream desire and hope—the fulness of joy and the substance of stone and life in any form. God is what makes less lonely the seeking human being who finds in you and me what we seek in others. Whatever your philosophy, or religion, if you relate only to it and fail to find or discern the implication of uniting with John and Joe and Mary, and Tom and Dick and Harry—and friend as well as foe—you will find nothing. Your religion, while not a fraud, will leave you wanting.

God is not a God of the dead but of the living. We've tried to justify our faith and prayed to win wars, overcome conditions and change people. It can't be done! And all we've done is obscure our vision, deepen the mist, and live unsatisfied lives in a turbulent world. You may agree there is a mist beyond which we have not seen. You may concur that the God most people pray to is so big and so far away that we are insignificant, and the voice we would speak is without sound. Yes God is big and far away. *But God is also infinitesimally small and very close: in every person, in every stone and grain of sand and fleck of dust.* You may assent to this but mere intellectual assent is not enough. We must still the mind, quiet the senses, close our eyes, and open our heart beyond ourselves. *But even this is not enough:* we must extend, expend and involve ourselves. Look around. What do you see? In one form or another you see matter and form and shape and life and substance in the clothes you wear, the thoughts you have, the air you breathe, your fellow man your hopes, dreams and aspirations. *Remove God from these and what and where is God?*

As long as we have been here, others have been with us, yet we have felt alone. We can be one with our fellow man and one with God. The choice is ours. The mist of our own making. And the solution? In one word: *Relate!*

WEEKLY PROGRAM
NUMBER

8

How to Loose Yourself from Confusing Thoughts Holding You Back

When the moon and the stars are beaming upon most men, then they have no need for things of the spirit, understanding, compassion, and relatedness—and it is at this time that their need is greatest. But when rainy days come and there is darkness at noon, when heart and soul seek out the spirit that is within, most men become "spiritual vagabonds." They seek, and seek, and seek—and do not find.

But a dreamy, peaceful afternoon that bestows its blessings and the breath of the breeze that imparts well-being can shorten the memory—for mind betokens self without the Self.

If each individual seeking God, purpose and meaning daily applied but a portion of the effort spend in time of desperation, the greatest of the world's great spiritual leaders would seem to be mere men among men—for the greatness of all would shine forth.

All that is misty in the world about us would lift as a fog dispelled by the bright and shining sun. But no, man would rather enclose reality with all that is not true. "It's difficult to discipline the self. I don't have time." You mean you won't be bothered! "And these disciplines—*Do they really work?*" You'll never know until you try.

I ask myself, "Why grope in darkness when there is the light of day?" And deep within, the answer comes, "It is for you to say, do, choose and be—whatever your heart, mind and soul would seek, or to ignore. But whatever it is you seek, do not deplore, for what you have is what you've sought and nothing more."

What do you seek, my friend, upon this path of fate? Fickle

59

foolishness and idle conversation? Or would your spirit be moved to take that first and faltering step to far free sky and open arms of all that God did give? Step forth! Fear not and know that what keeps you from your good is only yourself.

YOUR ASSIGNMENT FOR THIS WEEK

Now! You have a challenge. Decide to apply and put into practice the principles presented. We have talked of concentration. What is required of you is consecration. Consecrate yourself—mind, body and soul—to doing what heretofore has been but talk.

Relax, release, and let go of all that went before and all that is to be in your life. Concentrate upon this present moment. In this moment there is no room for despair, nor is it necessary to accept substitutes while striving for reality.

Within your mind create a tranquil scene. Give thanks to God. Breathe in deeply and hold the breath. As you breathe you are taking in the vital essence of life itself. Know this. Exhale. Inhale and hold to the count of twenty. Breathe out slowly to the count of twenty. In. Out. In. Out. And now return in thought to the tranquil scene created by the mind.

Concentrate on the only reality: Consecration. Let go. The spirit within will point the way. Allow the word itself, "Consecration," to be your guide in concentration. You will unfold and progress, as the spirit enfolds. *Observe the above as a daily discipline.*

Make note of what is outstanding that has been given you. Enscribe this in your working notebook. Mark the date.

> **"Keep thy heart with all diligence; for out of it are the issues of life." —Proverbs 4:23**

MAKE THIS—

YOUR DAILY AFFIRMATION FOR THE WEEK:

"The path to an evolving consciousness lies within me. Though I search over the face of this earth, I must return and look within. Everything that is without points to that which is within. I resolve to look within for the good I seek and to look upon everything as the good I seek."

The basis of reality
in daily living

The nature of man, God and spirit, in tender and gentle overture, whisper softly and proclaim, *"Do the best you can. Within you lies not only your hope and aspiration, but that which is good for you and good for other men. Within you lies the pattern, the plan and the way. No closed doors present themselves to you except those doors closed by you. Within others there is no opportunity for you except you accept as that which you seek. It lies in all others and in all things—when you learn awareness of that which is within the self."*
And Nature says yet more: *"If you would be no longer spiritually a vagabond, look deep within yourself, for therein lies the spirit of all that is. There is but one time to live—now! There is but one way to live—and in tenderness I say to you—*
"The path to an evolving consciousness lies within. Though you search over the face of this earth, you must return and look within. Everything that is outside you points to that which is within. Resolve to look within for the good you seek, and to look upon everything as the good you seek."

A step upon the path—

Long ago and far away a man had lost his way. Encountering an old man along the way, he asked of this fellow traveler (Socrates), "How can I reach Mr. Olympus?" Socrates answered, "Just make every step you take go in that direction." Wherever it is you would go—make every step take you in that direction. And now—another step—

Your self-development questions

Question 1. To feel an infinite spirit sustaining us during trial and tribulation is the great solace of mankind. *When one knows affliction and turns to the spirit, seeming not to find the comfort needed—what then shall that one do?*

Question 2. In all lands there are seasons of the year. In West and South the rain and drought are more common. In The North, Northwest and East, autumn ushers in a pageantry of color on the hill-sides as leaves turn to umber, flame and gold. *In all the various landscapes there is the treasure of the season. In things of the spirit there are no seasons—yet man remains a "spiritual vaga-bond" bereft of that which Nature gives so freely.* Why? Give careful consideration to your answer.

Question 3. We go on living and struggling while the world in which we live has much to give. We listen to the song of the bird, or the poet's inner theme—we hear the "Sound of Silence"—and yet we do not live. *With much that is so right, why is it there is so much that is so wrong?*

Question 4. Without a doubt we all seek the easy and gracious life. We strive to lessen our burdens and seek illumination of the spirit so that life may bestow its gifts upon us, and yet the greatest gifts of love, understanding and compassion, artistry and literature have come to us through those who have suffered grievously. Their art and interpretation came from life and its heartaches—that which they suffered, which none would have sought. *Why is it that those who suffer most return to life its best, and why the suffering for the giver of the gift?*

"Through faith we understand." —Hebrews 11:3

"STIMULATORS TO ACTION"—

Beginning today, make a resolution
   —just for today
And a fresh one for each day that follows—
That "I will spread happiness and joy and good to
   the first five people with whom I come in contact!"
As you do spread joy, happiness and good, you will find this increasing to overwhelming proportions, as your good, in overwhelming proportion, returns to you.

WEEKLY PROGRAM NUMBER

9

How to Know Your True Self

Time without end man has been adjured, admonished and besought to respond to all that is always and ever the best within himself and in other men. He knows all the words for all his wants: he knows the days of the week, the seasons of the year, and the years of his life. Yet he would rather have ideals without ideas and intention without application.

He says, "I desperately seek a way out of affliction," and then he whiles away untold opportunities to stand upon the stage of life and be himself. What is he? *The potential of all he would be.* And there is but one way for him to be what he would be: as he changes the clothes he wears, he must remove, exchange, and replace ideas within his mind which bring him less than the very best which life can give. Then by inspired bidding he will respond and be himself.

On rare occasions—in time of need—he will bare his soul. If he would really bare his soul and be himself, he must love when loving is not easy and give when he would rather receive. He must relate when mind and heart say loud and clear, "Depart," but a subtler and softer sound says, "Stay."

He knows what others may not know: that he is created in the image and likeness of God. He knows the importance of being loved, needed and wanted. Yet like an actor upon a stage, he wears a mask.

YOUR ASSIGNMENT FOR THIS WEEK

The first step in casting aside all that is an invention of and not an expression of the self is taken in the discipline of concentration—the action preceding greater unfoldment—*meditation*.

In concentration, *giving thought to a specific idea, the challenge is not in whether the discipline is good, but in knowing that directed concentration, spiritually oriented, is its own reward and a valid reason for the discipline.*

Important note: If you are satisfied with your life as it is, proceed no farther. If you would see the whole process of a better life unfolding within you, continue on.

Concentration is a conscious experience. It is neither mystical nor occult. It is but a means to further discernment of the self. It is the directing of your mind upon one specific idea of your choice. It must be made clear that concentration is not contemplation. It is consideration only of a part of the whole.

Now: With an unwavering conviction that you *will* be able to know God, proceed as directed in the seventh week's program. As you still the mind and body, preface your time of stillness with this thought, "I have come to this time and place to know God—first in myself, and then in all things. I am calm, peaceful and serene. I allow the spirit to direct what I will discern."

Hold to the thought that comes to you. Make no attempt to understand its essence. Accept it and exclude all other thoughts. Let this be God's gift to you. In turn, it will by your gift to others.

Observe the preceding as a daily discipline.

Record that which has been revealed to you.

"Take away the dross from the silver, and there shall come forth a vessel for the finer." —Proverbs 25:4

MAKE THIS—

YOUR DAILY AFFIRMATION FOR THE WEEK:

"My true identity is one with God and with my fellow man. This day, this week, I make every effort to be that which I am—a warmer expression of love, and a deeper experience of oneness with all with whom I have the blessed privilege of coming in contact."

Your basis of reality
in today's living

Every one of us, without exception, is God-like. Every one of us desires a better relationship with others. Yet we hide behind an infinite wardrobe of disguises: we obscure identity behind a thousand masks.

Greatness, goodness and God-likeness is the substance and sustenance of every living creature, and yet to release that which we are we must accept that which is great, God-like and good in ourselves and in others. To do this we must lift and love our fellow man where inclination would have us do anything but this. From a practical point of view this is the only alternative to chaotic thinking and distortion of life.

"My true identity is one with God and with my fellow man. This day, this week, I make every effort to be that which I am—a warmer expression of love, and a deeper experience of oneness with all with whom I have the blessed privilege of coming in contact."

A time for participation—

"Ancient Jewish tradition insists that no performance is complete without the participation of the heart. It asks for "Kavanah"—inner participation—not only external action." —Abraham Joshua Herschel
Man's Quest for God

Your self-development questions

Question 1. Man makes a mystery of himself: he constructs the disguise wherein he defeats the purpose of his purpose. John Donne, the poet of long ago (1573-1631), shared an insight which can be of meaning to us:

"He brought light out of darkness, not out of a lesser light; he can bring thy summer out of winter, though thou have no spring; though in the ways of fortune or understanding or conscience, thou have been benighted til now, wintered and frozen, clouded and eclipsed, damped and benumbed, smothered and stupefied till now, now God comes to

thee, not as in the dawning of the day, not as in the bud of the spring, but as the sun at noon."

How will an understanding of this lift the veil of deception of the self?

Question 2. Religion is the first step in any direction. Though this is true, *why has religion failed so many?*

Question 3. Many who follow religion, mysticism and the varied paths of spiritual life are merely seeking an escape. Escapism is but another disguise preventing the truth of an individual from being expressed. *When there have been many who have proved the importance of discarding the mask of concealment, why are so many reluctant to give up a counterfeit life?*

Question 4. The relationship between right ideas, good health, vital living and meaningful objectives is more than coincidence. Most of us know this. Yet we are held captive by the excuse of "the age, the socity and the time in which I live." *Though there are hard and fast rules for freeing ourselves from the bondage of ignorance and the chains of self-imposed restriction, in what way will you discard whatever false appearance prevents others from knowing you as you think, feel, hope and strive?*

"And he shall find all that he can ask, and that as deep as the mind of man is able to reach." —Jacob Boehme, 1575-1624

"STIMULATORS TO ACTION"—

Listen to raindrops upon a window pane.
Beyond the sound of rain upon a window
there is a deeper sound—and sense—of nature.
Look upon your fellow man. More than eye beholds—
there is a deeper depth.
If you are able to look upon and listen to more than
sight and sound alone,
You will be moved to feel. And as you feel,
you will be moved to act.
"Commune with your own heart . . . " —Psalm 4:4

WEEKLY PROGRAM
NUMBER

10

How to Stop Dreaming and Start Producing Benefits for Yourself

In the lessons given and in those which follow you are given practical procedures to apply during the week. There are several important considerations:

1. God *is* the underlying foundation for every physical, material, psychological and spiritual reality.
2. The books of the Bible are an assemblage of practical instruction and precepts for successful, meaningful and productive living.
3. A partial acceptance of the principles presented will not work.
4. You will learn, *"There is no weak-kneed doctrine called truth."* You will *know that truth is a powerful, dynamic force with which you direct your life.*

As you proceed you will learn how to pray and in the process understand that prayer is the least understood of all the powers known to man. You will learn the meaning of meditation and the measure and means of entering the Silence.

There is but one purpose here—to help you live an abundant, creative life; to make you a more effective person, the best person you are able to be—on *all* levels of your being—*physical, mental and spiritual. TO DEVELOP YOUR OWN INNATE POTENTIAL.*

"By their fruits ye shall know them" —Matthew 7:20

And now: Let us take Jesus at His word:

67

"What things soever ye desire, when ye pray, BELIEVE that ye receive them and ye shall have them" —Mark 11:24

This is one of the great lessons of life: " . . . unto you as you believe."

A first step; a beginning principle—

One of the first principles of prosperity, peace of mind, well-being, understanding, compassion or relatedness is "sharing." So in these lessons, plan on having a friend join with you—someone with whom you can actively progress on that which is indigenous to inner growth.

MAKE THIS—

YOUR DAILY AFFIRMATION FOR THE WEEK:

"I stop dreaming of good and start producing good!"

The basis of reality in daily living

"Today I am going to PROVE my beliefs in the supremacy of spirit and its action in my life, as LIFE, HEALTH, and PROSPERITY! I am showing to the world my true understanding of truth, and I prove it by speaking and doing only that which is positive and productive. I will end this day and this week knowing that to the best of my ability I have been faithful in proving my trust in the truth to which I have been exposed."

"I stop dreaming of good and start producing good!"

YOUR ASSIGNMENT FOR THIS WEEK

POINTS TO REMEMBER

Realize: Words of wisdom are without meaning unless they become a living experience, always renewed from day to day.

Daily: Join with at least one other person and read Chapter Five of the Book of Matthew (the beginning of the Sermon on the Mount). Discuss what you have read, seeking to find the meaning behind each word. Note: A good companion book for a deeper understanding is "The Sermon on the Mount," by Emmet Fox.

Now: In the words of the Psalmist, *"Be still and know that I am God." —Psalm 46:10*

Observe: *A period of silence.*

"I will say to them which were not my people, Thou art my people; and they shall say, Thou art my God." —Hosea 2:23

How Ivan, "at the end of his rope" from drinking and little education, raised himself to success

Perhaps you are familiar with the problem of drinking to the point where you no longer desire food, friends or associates—only a drink. Perhaps you have reached the point where drink itself was no longer a solace but a necessity—*and it tore your insides out* with violent inner turmoil and the desperation of being the loneliest person in the world—for though you no longer eat or have friends, you do desire desperately to have another human reach out with heart and hand and accept you as you are—for you would not be as you are.

Such a man was Ivan. He had reached the end of his rope, the bottom of the barrel. There was nowhere to go. I remember the first time I saw this man. He impressed me. Although he had been drinking, he seemed sober—in a way perhaps more sober than I, for he knew his own desperation. He didn't say much except, "Can you help me?" I liked his looks. And though I learned later that he was not an educated man, he was an articulate man with a superb mind, but a man who felt he was nothing and that he had nowhere to go—except straight to hell. In this case it was a personal hell of hell called *shoel,* or the grave. Yet there remained one spark of hope: his words, "Can you help me?" Here he was, looking up from the bottom of the deepest pit into which one can be thrust, saying "Can you help me?"

I looked at him for a long time. "How much do you want help? How much do you *really* want help?" He returned my look. "Dear God, man. Would I be here if I didn't want help? Would I? No!" I let him talk. There was no need to draw him out. That which he told me has been the heartache of untold thousands. I knew it was unnecessary to know the reasons, conditions and circumstances which may have brought him to this moment of truth.

After nearly three hours of his talking and my listening, he asked me the question to which his heart cried out for an answer: "Can you help me? Can you help me: If you can, will you, knowing what you know about me? You certainly cannot respect me, can you?" My heart went out to this man. "I will do whatever I can. But mostly, it will be to share with you a way in which you can help yourself. I'll be there to take your hand, but you will have to put your feet upon the path. Are you desperate enough to make the attempt?" He was. But he also needed more than someone telling him that it could be done—he had to be shown, helped, assisted every step of the way.

Pointing out to Ivan that there are principles governing every aspect of life, of this universe and of the individual, I also pointed out that these principles cannot be ignored. Nor can we apply a partial principle. Our dedication to that which we would have in our lives, rather than to that which we would no longer have, must be complete. His emphasis, his life, his desperation, were bound by haunting memories, memories of a past that extended to this very moment. He understood this as I asked him a question. "Ivan, I know much about alcoholism. I may even be considered an authority on drinking, and yet you are the real expert. If I came to you, and in the light of your own personal experience, asked your help, what would you tell me? How would you advise me? What would you give me to do, to say, to think, to be?" The look that came over his face was far from pensive. "You know! I think I've got the answer.

"I know I've got the answer! But I'll need your help. The first thing I would tell you to do is to 'hold' to what you want—forget the damnable memories that haunt and drive one crazy. HOLD TO WHAT YOU ARE SEEKING! That is the one way in which I know I can help myself and I pray that I can be of help to others in this same position. I know I can—I won't even ask you if you believe in me, for, for the first time, *'I've found the answer.' "*

With little help from me, other than knowing that I was there in case he faltered, Ivan proceeded to embrace principles that will not vary for any man—and yet will work effectively for whoever will make the dedication completely and totally. Today Ivan, though he lacks even a high school education, holds down a responsible (and rewarding) position, making $12,000 a year as counselor-therapist to those faced with what had been a problem to him.

WEEKLY PROGRAM
NUMBER
11
The Powers of Desire

It seems unnecessary to state, that if man wanted something sufficiently, he would have it. A more reasonable assumption would be that while one earnestly desires something, he may just not know how to go about achieving or acquiring it—or, for that matter, evolving it.

On this theory, let us proceed to consider the manner and means of evolving. Assuming that *you* really desire something, settle within your mind what it is you really want: knowledge of God, better human relationships, personal growth, understanding of a situation, increased income, health, a better personality or whatever.

Regardless of designation, what you are seeking is that which you have determined will give your life meaning and will result in happiness.

It becomes important now to accept the fact that it is possible to bring into your life that which you hold within your mind. How you do this and to what extent depends entirely upon you. The results will be directly proportional to the degree of diligence with which you pursue your goal—results will equal efforts.

It also becomes extremely important to accept that strain and struggle is a distraction keeping us from that which we seek. Perhaps we can best understand what is being said in this light: I wish to transform or change something from what it is into what it is not. Or; there is something I want which I now do not have. I can struggle to think of one or a thousand ways to bring this to me. All this requires effort. But there is another approach. I can release, completely and totally, this overwhelming desire—relax and allow that which I seek to come through a mind free of extraneous thoughts, erratic wandering. This is what we shall do.

YOUR ASSIGNMENT FOR THIS WEEK

In our effort to evolve, memories of the past and hopes for the future complicate our ability to concentrate on the present. We are forever in the middle of a muddle. We know we must give thought to that which is at hand. Our mind returns to a time in the past and reaches forth toward an indefinite future. We must live and concern ourselves with the present. We must concentrate on that which is at hand.

The key and the capstan of the soul is concentration—the ability to meet at one point and bring into focus renewed strength by removal of foreign elements which keep one from forming ideas at a common center.

Now: Allow your mind to rise to lofty heights. Let it rise to an area bereft of atmosphere and all else. Extend it forth in all directions. Leave behind all thought of past, present and future. For a moment, rest peacefully in the tranquility.

With your mind spread wide and far and unencumbered, give thought to that idea determined earlier. Through expansion of the mind, you now concentrate your total mind on that which you seek. Focus on this and nothing else. Approach, embrace and become one with what you have sought. Let this be in your mind, your being, your power, and your presence. You and it are one! There is none else. *If this has happened, it would be not a pebble at your feet, but a world encompassed—Not a fleck of dust upon the air, but an understanding relationship—not a man or being separate from you. The knowledge that you sought would be yours now: all else, ethereal unreality and memories haunting him, who holds to past and seeks beyond the now.*

Document revelation and what this means to you.

"This gospel of the kingdom shall be preached in all the world."
—Matthew 24:14

MAKE THIS—

YOUR DAILY AFFIRMATION FOR THE WEEK:

"I release the past. I release the future. My consideration is with the present—this moment—this day!"

Your self-development questions

Our minds are powerful instruments for accomplishment. What we accomplish is that to which we have given our attention. Dwell in the past and we achieve little in the present. Fondly anticipate the future without thought to the present, and we circumvent and beguile that which we may consumate now or later. There is but one way to reach a goal: by the effort we put forth now. Every consideration must orient itself toward that goal—now.

Yes, our minds are powerful instruments for accomplishment. What is it you would accomplish? What would you have that you do not have at this moment? Think about it; dream about it. Let it become part, not of what you would be, or have, or do, but of what you are at this moment. Each day this week, declare, believe, accept: *"I release the past. I release the future. My consideration is with the present—this moment—this day."*

Consider this: for there is no other way—

"Be not conformed to this world: but be ye transformed by the renewing of your mind, that ye may prove what is that good, and acceptable, and perfect, will of God." —Romans 12:2

Question 1. You have a mind, spirit and body that are wonderful beyond comprehension. *State specific steps to be taken in the development and expression of your mind, body and affairs.*

Question 2. The principle of continuity is the foundation of comparative psychology. The most basic and important of psychological inquiry is the science of the study of human behavior. *Accepting the premise that thought has a continuity to it, why is it so very difficult for most individuals to concentrate on a specific* *subject, without thoughts rambling and turning to concepts far removed from the original intent?*

Question 3. J. Krishnamurti, in his book *The First and Last Freedom*, states: " . . . there is a vast difference between awareness and . . . introspection. Introspection leads to frustration, to further and greater conflict; whereas awareness is a process of release from the action of the self . . . You observe without condemnation, without identification; therefore in that observation there is complete communion . . . This actually takes place when you are deeply, profoundly interested in something." *All of us are interested in a greater awareness and communion with God, our fellow man, nature, and our own inner spirit. How would* you *reduce the effort required to establish this exchange with man, Nature, and God?*

Question 4. On the basis of available evidence, i.e. observable behavior, we can conclude that, although most humans give many reasons for their behavior, their efforts are usually to resolve one issue: that of meaning for the individual. *Knowing that everyone desires greater meaning in life, state what you believe to be the way to achieve this meaning.*

> **"How is it then, brethren? when ye come together, every one of you hath a psalm, a doctrine, hath a tongue, hath a revelation, hath an interpretation. Let all things be done unto edifying."**
> **—I Corinthians 14:26**

"STIMULATORS TO ACTION"—

Create an image within your mind
of something bigger and better in your life.
Accept only that which will enrich the life
of another.
Affirm to yourself, "This I do believe!—
This I will achieve!"
Determine
to affirm and reaffirm
a hundred times a day.
By affirmation there will be confirmation—
and—
Stimulation to Action!

Mindful of that which is sought—a pertinent observation that follows.

"What is health?"

In his lifetime man asks many questions. One perplexing question he fails to ask is, "What is health?" He may ask, "Why has this happened to me? Why am I ill? What is the cause, the reason?" Rarely does he ask, "What is health? How do I have it? What must I do?"

When he "feels well" he gives little thought as to why he "happens" to be well. *He doesn't "happen" to be well, to have health. He is healthy for the same reason he is sick, discouraged, distraught, fearful or out of order.* The very same principle which makes him less than he can and would be *will make him more than he is.* This principle of "mind action" may be likened to a vast body of water, a forested mountain, or a cloud in the sky. In proper perspective, each serves a function. On occasion, however, each can hold disaster. The body of water can nourish, sustain, enrich and add immeasurably to life as a haven for the weary and a beautiful and renewing sight for all who would behold it. *Water can also drown, innundate and devastate.* A forested mountain can be a sanctuary for every form of life and freedom for the harassed. *It can be a frightening wilderness to one who is lost, and a source of danger to the careless.* A cloud in the sky? Of God, creation's purest beauty! Of man? Pollution. Hiroshima. Nagasaki. Man asks many questions and seeks few answers.

What is health? Some seem to think it is the absence of sickness. If this were the case we could say that health was intelligence, for sickness can be the result of ignorance. However the most intelligent of men have known great illness. So although illness *is* ignorance, health is neither intellect nor education. *Health is a mind attuned to the power of the universe—Attuned to and productive of that which is harmonious.* Though there may be harmony or disharmony in the universe, we are always drawing upon this power. How we use this power determines sickness or health, well-being or frustration, abundance or lack. It is your business and mine to know how to properly utilize that which belongs to every man or suffer inexorably until we do.

One may unknowingly and unwittingly experience great physical harm by grasping a naked wire. One may, in ignorance, suffer illness or want. One does not "happen" to have, experience, or know health. Around us, abundantly and constantly, nature expresses health and order. Man knows what produces a verdant crop, a luxuriant treè, or a clean atmosphere. He also "knows" that health is the activity of the mind in attunement with self, others, the environment and the universe.

Who is health for?

If for even a moment one should think that health is for the chosen few, should he not consider that providence then must place a cross upon the shoulders of the unwary? If you and I are to know the meaning of health, we must understand the reason for ill health—encompassing all areas of mind, body, and affairs. Sickness, whether of the mind, body or affairs, is *patterned wrong thinking and incorrect living, resulting in continued exposure to situations we are unable to resolve.* Both sickness and health conform to a pattern. The power to produce health or disorder remains the same—within the mind. We can readily agree there is such a condition as "illness" in the world. We see ample evidence of this in the minds and bodies of many, in the increasing number of hospitals and hospitalized, in the vast disorder in our environment, endless wars, in the heart-felt need of alcoholics, and among the young with drug abuse. We can readily agree that there are such conditions as disorder, inharmony, and frustration. This is sickness: ignorance and abandonment of principles producing order and harmony.

The power of positive health

If we can agree that there is a condition called disorder we can surely agree there is a condition of conduct recognizable as health, order, peace, harmony, well-being, happiness, and good—a God-like condition. The healing capacity either exists or it does not. *And it does exist! Healing rests upon confidence in and acceptance of the underlying principle of healing.* As long as fear, doubt and hesitation are eliminated, as long as we accept this healing power with every fiber of our being, our minds, bodies, and affairs will corroborate and testify to healing. Failing to accept and embrace will bring a testament of disorder! Into the affairs of our minds and bodies we can inject the highest concept of God—or the lowest expression of man. The power of the spirit and the choice of each of us lies within our own minds. The divine mind is not selective; we are. The divine mind works at the level of our projection: acceptance or rejection. We rely upon it to heal and to make life beneficent and "It" will do for us only what we will do with it. The fundamental principle of healing is: Divine saturation of every area of mind, body, and affairs with the power of the spirit—in a spiritual manner.

While it becomes important to caution those with spiritual leanings not to become sanctimonious about the knowledge they think they have of God, spirit, and spiritual things, it becomes of equal importance to admonish those whose impious demeanor rejects the mention of God. The determining factor in health is a receptive mind, open to the actuality of the healing process. We talk "about" health, order, harmony, abundance, and happiness. It is clearly evident that we must do more than talk. So now let us begin to do something with our minds. We have spoken of concentration. By definition, "concentration" is a narrowing, a reduction, a making small. "Spiritual concentration" which we do with both the mind and spirit, makes whole and encompasses all.

For a concentrated healing process, expand your mind to encompass all that is life-giving—trees, ideas, goodness, people. Dwell on these things. During this coming week agree that there is a condition of conduct recognizable as order, health, peace, well-being, happiness, good, and God-likeness. Then make an effort, a genuine effort, to express and experience an expansion of the healing spirit, through concentration upon all that is God-like—*for all is God!*

How Tom raised himself from frustration and self-pity to health, wealth and happiness

There is little doubt in my mind but that every man and woman on the face of this earth desires a feeling of well-being, health, peace of mind, and the good things in life. And yet how few indeed have any of these things except for a fleeting, passing moment!

In any discussion of "health," it is soon recognized that health involves "prosperity," and it is shortly observed that prosperity does bring some sense of peace of mind and does "buy" many of the good things of life. Now, knowing that "health" is the door behind which all of these things are locked, what and where is the key?

The key to health lies within you and me and all of us. The key is our attitude of mind. And our attitude of mind is an attitude of acceptance or rejection of self. How few of us accept ourselves for what we really are or for what we *really can be!* We are governed by the attitudes of others: our lives are determined by what we think others will think of us and we seldom risk standing on the edge of the precipice for fear of falling off. Thus we miss the grandeur of the view of what lies before us. That we do just exactly this and miss the best of life is best illustrated by considering how synonymous are the conditions of our mind, body, and affairs with what we have conditioned ourselves to accept that is a rejection of self.

Tom placed the blame on circumstances, conditions, people, and events—everything under the sun—for *his* ill health, the *disturbance* he had and was experiencing, and *the* "poor" salary and job he had. I asked him what kind of person he thought he was. "Well!" he said, with indignation in his voice, "I know what I am and I know who I am. It's just that nobody else seems to know *my* worth." I sat there opposite him for about fifteen minutes without comment. Then I said, "Tom, you've told me that you *know* what and who you are. *What are you? And who are you? And what is your worth?*" There was noticeable reaction. What I said and projected determined *his* actions and attitudes, and he didn't like what I was saying. This unhappy, unhealthy and mis-directed human being must have experienced this same thing for all too long.

"I'll tell you, Tom, *what* you are, *who* you are, and what you are *worth.* You are a lonely, frustrated, heartsick individual. *Who* are you? You are no different than I—except in your expression of what you would be. You want the same things I do—*except for you, somehow or other, they just don't seem to have come to you.*

What is your worth? Most of us never really know because we will not think our own thoughts. We would rather talk than act. We would rather complain than constructively contribute to our own well-being. What is *your* worth? I would ask you this: would you stop talking long enough to listen? Not to me, but to something within yourself that tells you who you are, what you are, and why. If you like, I will share with you what has been shared with me, through the great minds and the inspiration that was theirs— not in thought, but in actual, living, vital, vibrant experience."

It would be difficult to say exactly what Tom's reaction was. Though inscrutable, he was not insensitive. I could see that it was difficult for him, *but he did listen.* "What is it I would share with you that has been shared with me? I'd have to tell you, as these minds of other men spoke to me:

> Walk along the razor's edge. Help others in whatever way you are able. But pay no heed to what others may think of you or your actions so long as you know your actions are right. Depart from yourself and pursue "the" course of life. Look beyond where you stand. Listen to the sound not heard with the ear alone. Rise from lowly resting place and hold within your heart and hand the heart of that which appears to be just a stone. Be yourself! Be not fashioned according to another's dream but dream and fashion your own high and lofty dream.

Tom listened and *heard* not the words I uttered, but the singleness of individuality and the meaning that means growing "together." Today I see a familiar face where in the past I saw a "stranger unto himself." Today Tom lives a far different life than he used to. He has the same job, but he makes a lot more money and has far more responsibility than he did. He lives in the same house, but he lives a far different life than he did. He is a happy, healthy, well-oriented man, and if you were to ask him who he was, without hesitation he would reply, "I am the richest man in the world. Not in money, but I have all I need. I never worry. I'm healthy. And I think human beings are the greatest people in the world." *Something happened to him. It can happen to you if you follow the programs in this book.*

What Health Is and How to Achieve It

12

In moments of illumination most of us sense that conditions of life as we have known them are far below the level intended. Born of the spirit greater than most of us experience, common sense tells us we should be healthy and can aspire to peace of mind; logic seems to say "you need not know need."

No one would deny that health is life and that life is a vibrant, living truth. If we are to know health and the meaning of health we must live up to the highest truth, an expression of life at its fullest.

In defining health as in truth, definitions seem inadequate. As we cannot experience truth in words alone, neither can we know health by verbalization but rather by demonstration. We can demonstrate health by one means only: Knowing the truth of our being and being that truth. In the simplest language: *Know that God is the source of health, peace of mind, and prosperity, and attune ourselves with God.* Again, we do this in one way only: Walk, talk, eat, sleep, drink, dream, and practice the presence of God's Goodness.

WHAT HEALTH REALLY IS

Health is not so much a state of mind as a condition of being—being in tune with the man on the corner, the stone in the field, the water in the stream—with God in the universe. Health is the music in every sound, the song of the bird, the intelligence of

81

your mind, and the spirit you express. Health is a declaration of the presence of God in every cell of your body and the acknowledgement of this presence in all you understand and in that which you neither comprehend nor appreciate. Health is knowing that every cell of every form of life is completely entwined with this presence. We have no need to seek health or healing. We should recognize that beyond its appearance our natural condition is one with the Divine, and that sickness of mind, body, or affairs is an expression of our own acceptance.

You would know health?

Affirm: *"My mind, body, and affairs, all that I experience, all with whom I come in contact, and each condition and circumstance, is spiritual substance and cannot be limited nor limiting in any way. I now consciously direct my every thought to the remembrance of the truth of my being. I rejoice in perfect fulfillment."*

YOUR ASSIGNMENT FOR THIS WEEK

In time of quiet contemplation consider the meaning embodied in the above affirmation. You are being exposed to what is the standard of life—recognition of life and your part in it.

Now: Turn completely away from your former way of thinking, not by a deliberate effort to shut out old forms, but by concentration on a new and productive means of healthful expression of perfection—acknowledging the healing presence *within.*

Consciously accept and expect your mind, body, and affairs to respond to the strength of the power of your affirmation.

Quietly spend fifteen minutes daily in reading and meditation upon spiritual things.

Repeat the affirmation. Learn it. Make it part of your every thought.

"My mind, body and affairs, all that I experience, all with whom I come in contact, and each condition and circumstance is spiritual substance and cannot be limited nor limiting in any way. I now consciously direct my every thought to the remembrance of this truth of my being. I rejoice in perfect fulfillment."

Thank God *in all your attitudes toward others and toward all things.*

"I will work a work in your days, which ye will not believe, though it be told you." —Habakkuk 1:5

MAKE THIS—

YOUR DAILY AFFIRMATION FOR THE WEEK:

"I realize that God is where I am. Realizing that God is life, I know that the healing power of God is present in me and in all that concerns me. I give grateful thanks."

Your basis of reality in daily living

How evident is the healing power present in the universe! I lay hands on myself and without benefit of thought or effort on my part, *I am healed!*

Though the field of medicine has attracted the most brilliant of minds and has made tremendous strides in many fields of research, *healing still takes place within the individual.* With deep respect for and recognition of the importance of men of medicine, *no man heals another.* Man may not know this and may deny the presence of a universal power of healing, but this changes not that power. It does, however, reduce one's ability to experience the healing he would have.

"I realize that God is where I am. Realizing that God is life, I know that the healing power of God is present in me and in all that concerns me. I give grateful thanks."

"I shall yet praise him, who is the health of my countenance, and my God." —Psalm 42:11

Enlightened truth—

You will only live your life to its fullest potential when you consciously decide to follow a discipline oriented toward expressing that potential.

Your self-development questions

Question 1. Should another tell you that he "heard" voices directing him to act in a certain manner or to do a certain thing, you might not believe him. Certainly some would doubt his sanity. In the Book of Isaiah, Chapter 30, Verse 21, we read, *"And thine ears shall hear a word behind thee, saying, This is the way, walk ye in it, when ye turn to the right hand, and when ye turn to the left." Why should we accept this scripture and reject the word of another telling us that he heard a voice?*

Question 2. In Matthew 10:32, we read, *"Whosoever therefore shall confess me before men, him will I confess also before my Father which is in heaven." What does this "confession" of Christ mean? And how does one confess Christ?*

Question 3. If healing is a universal force, available to all, why is there so much evidence to the contrary?

Question 4. Basic and important to all we do is a time of prayer. *According to your understanding of prayer, will you set aside a few moments each day to join with another in prayer? If the answer is affirmative, set the time.*

> "Whatsoever we ask, we receive of him, because we keep his commandments, and do those things . . . [which are to be done]." —I John 3:22

"STIMULATORS TO ACTION"—

Take a positive, dynamic idea such as:
"I am alive, alert, awake, joyous and enthusiastic!"
Repeat this aloud forty or fifty times—
Until it becomes a deeply ingrained habit of thinking.
The next day formulate another positive, dynamic idea.
Habitize it.
You will have become the idea you have conceived.

How a woman found her purpose in life

"The champion race horse—smooth, sleek, and beautiful—and a woman compared to this exquisitely beautiful creature are created for a purpose." This thought once occurred to me.

A woman once said to me, "How much a woman can be likened to a race horse! Not every woman—but some. They can be a delight to behold, sensitive, tense, nervous, and aware. Everything about them exudes a sensation that is exhilarating, exciting and sometimes unpredictable. Some are winners; others, no matter how beautiful are losers. I wonder what purpose a race horse has for living? And what is my own purpose for existence? A plough-horse I can understand. It is a beast of burden and built to withstand the pressures upon it. I wonder if there is a purpose for either a beautiful woman—or a race horse?"

I smiled, thinking to myself, "I'm sure many would have a far different perspective than mine." I answered her question, "To inspire men."

"To what?" "I wonder just how much a horse—or a woman—can inspire a man? I used to think *I* could inspire others. Let's talk about the plough-horse. It doesn't seem to have a will of its own. It does what its master makes it do—by beating, whipping, or cajoling it. The fate of some domesticated animals is sad. But we both know its purpose apparently was *not* that of the horse fashioned to other than the plow. *I feel more like a plough-horse.* Watch it: It can be in a field, perfectly free, and the wind and the rain and the lightening have little effect upon it—it hardly even raises its head. I don't believe anyone can ever break the will of a race horse, or a truly wild and free animal of nature: it would rather be destroyed first. But how much greater the suffering must be for the thoroughbred! Right now I feel like a pack horse, a beast of burden—something I *never* was meant to be. We hear constantly about "opportunities." What good is a race horse if it isn't in a race, or if it doesn't win? Is the competition alone enough? I don't believe it, for all of life is competitive—and who wins? Even the one who seems to win winds up with ulcers, a heart attack, a broken home, disturbed and distraught. And when it's all over, what's the purpose? What's the purpose of *my* existence? You tell me, and I don't think I'll believe you even after you've told me. What is the purpose of *my* existence? I'm tied down, unhappy, feeling like I haven't accomplished anything. I live and die—a beautiful nobody."

Though she didn't really seem to be expecting an answer, I replied, "I'll ask *you* a question. What is a beautiful woman? A beautiful race horse? Beauty of any kind? Accomplishment? *It is* that subtle "something" unseen and sensed by all too few. It is that moment when you know that we are friends. It is the bark upon a tree; the twist and turn of trunk and bending limb; the change, almost imperceptible, in an ever-changing cloud, the sound of a newborn babe; early morning dew; smoke from a campfire; the smell of pine; a shaft of sunlight breaking the depth of darkness, giving shadows darker hues and beauty to me and you. An appreciation of this, however great or small, is an accomplishment, and the beauty of this accomplishment is the worth and meaning of your life and mine. More important, these are the very things we seek—harmony, peace of mind, a sense of worth, and understanding of meaning. Beauty is in all these things. But how do we achieve, recognize, and experience them?" This woman had been speaking of beauty and women and race horses and of a plough-horse—and, in a deeper sense, of her own personal anguish. What was her problem? Most certainly a loss of any sense of personal worth—*and of freedom.* She knew that she *must have some value.* Her mind was disturbed and filled with emotion, and she knew no peace.

But my thoughts were not of a thoroughbred, but of a pack-horse, and of a diary written nearly a century ago—and how it applied to this woman. The writer of long ago observed his humble pack-horse and a herd of wild horses and noted:

"How many times in my travels have I observed the wild beauty of a stallion leading his herd. And many times have I considered the nature of these animals free. And then, in looking at my faithful pack-horse, the thought, 'What a different breed.' He's burdened, yes. But, remove the burden, let him rest a few days, and he is still a pack-horse. How wrong I was. And thus I lost a good animal. Somehow, though I lost this trusted and most needed of animals, I knew a deeper sense of meaning in my own life as a result of what happened to him.

"How many times I have observed the wild beauty of a stallion leading his herd. For several days the 'herd' had come closer and closer to camp. This particular day I had loose tethered 'Stoney.' I noticed some edginess about him and had considered this a fear of the other horses. Not concerned, I paid little heed, going about minding my own business. Just before dusk on the night before, I had seen the dust of running horses and heard the thundering of hooves. Now, as I went down to water and care for my pack horse, I found the tether stake, rope, and him—gone. The next time I saw him it was a sight to behold; there he was, standing on the rise of a small hill, nostrils flared, head held high, tail blowing in the wind—for all the world, as wild and proud as those with whom he ran. This no longer was a beast of burden; here was God's magnificent beauty, free of all that would have destroyed that beauty. In my sadness at losing him, I knew an overwhelming sense of joy at the prospect of what he now had become, and I knew that what he had become, he must have been all the time."

I shared this story with the one who had brought it back to mind. And, in the telling of it, a new light shone from her eyes. "Do you suppose you could point the way for me—not to run with a wild herd—but to lift my head high, and know the spirit of freedom from all that has bound me for so very long?"

I need not tell you of the changes in this woman—except to say, thanks to the program she followed, she truly is an object of beauty—with most of her life, whatever the circumstance, one of standing upon *"the high hill"* of *"inner expression!"*

The unknown key to lasting health

In any consideration of health and healing, the interest is usually centered around sickness and lack of health. Rather than what we would have, our thoughts are on that which we would be rid of. In these disciplines our concern has little to do with illness, the particular condition, or even what may have been the cause: it is devoted, rather, to that of which health, healing, and wholeness will be the end result rather than its consequence. Our interest is *how to achieve, establish, and maintain health*— not how to eliminate sickness or get rid of something we don't want.

When we are not whole, too often we ask: "Why?" "Why am I sick? Why has this happened?" We are asking the wrong questions. Of greater value to us is the knowledge of *how to have* health, peace of mind, and all else we might have the right to seek. We might say that healing is a state of mind and a discipline adhered to—but it is more than this. Words are more than articulated sound; words upon a piece of paper are more than the paper of which they are part. They are the *whole* of the one who uttered them and *part* of all who listen. Words are repositories of the spirit of mind and man—and God. Yes, words are more than words, and healing is more than a state of mind and a discipline adhered to. *Healing is the process of a burning commitment and dedication of oneself to the unique simplicity of the truth we seek to know. Healing is a process of change.*

The importance of acceptance

In healing there is no static of the mind or body. Acceptance implies rejection: by acceptance of what we would have, there is rejection of what we would no longer have. Life and healing is movement, renewal—a gradual or spontaneous activity. And some, in sickness, do not live, until they die. Not in a physical sense—but to all the misconceptions that have concealed, hidden and thrust beyond reach the subdued voice of Him who asked, *"Wilt thou be made whole?"* If our answer is truly yes, we are born to a new spirit and a new awareness that we have words for the most profound and simplest of ideas.

We know! Knowledge becomes intuitive—our tongue is tied. But we have gained a foothold on the threshold of God, and know the meaning of healing and wholeness. We do not turn health on nor do we turn healing off. We are not well or sick: *we are God-like, or less than that which we were meant to be.*

What you want for yourself?

Healing is evolving toward the goal of God. *Wholeness is God!* A concept of health, an understanding of healing, and a knowledge of wholeness are nothing more and something less than thoughts within the mind of man who knows *not* the dimension of God and the demeanor of himself.

What good is this knowledge if one will not "will" beyond the condition to a devotion? He pours his precious hopes into an abyss. We are on a pilgrimage through life. Some of the most precious yearnings of your heart and mine deny the depth of our quest. In our minds we weave a garland of roses and find that in reality we've woven weeds. You would have health and wholeness? *"Wilt thou be made whole?"* On this journey through life, health is not an end but a never-ending beginning! Join with me now—where health, healing and wholeness are more than words and each word is a volume—in prayer. We still the mind, relax the body, and make our total being receptive to the source of the soul. In our minds we seek—but not by frustrated striving—*health and all that it implies.* In our words we seek the expansiveness of a language and the power to be more than we have been. In our hearts we yield—and in our powerlessness we know the fulness of all power. We speak of health healing, wholeness, harmony, and order. *Let us listen in silence and know that the "light" we seek in the dark, must burn within to burst forth, and that which we seek is that which we are.* We who grope in the darkness are the very light we seek.

How to dedicate yourself

Let us start with a personal concern. Release it. Select your own "retreat." Health? Peace? To be worthy of all I seek and seek all of which I am worthy? *Union with God?* This demands of me an intensity and a dedication to things of the spirit—wherein I lose all power to decry, disclaim, and decree—and all that remains is *the power to be!* I am like one who works for pay—but in the joy of that which I passionately do, the subtle sound of God is my reward. I lose sight of even that which I have sought and become that which I seek. *"Wilt thou be made whole? Wilt thou be made whole? Wilt thou be made whole?"*

WEEKLY PROGRAM
NUMBER
13

How to Have the Power of Healing

If I would have health I must identify with that which produces health. This necessitates two observations and one perspective.

The first observation: A doctrine of identification.

The second observation: That everyone and everything is an instrument through which health becomes a reality.

My perspective now assumes a communal aspect. The nature of my perception is: in all situations and with all I possess, I relate in a manner conducive to health and healing. Where there exists disharmony or discord, I contribute spiritually constructive attitudes. *I am that balance I seek.*

The mendacity of understanding produces illness where health is sought; disturbance rather than peace; frustration instead of fulfillment; and the eking out an existence in lieu of abundance.

Neither Moses nor Jesus nor any of "the spirits of the spirit" were concerned with initiating a new cult. They sought to stimulate others to the creative spirit of an understanding of self, God, and the individual's relationship to his community. Each taught that which we seek. Each found that which is sought. We symbolize rather than becoming the symbol. We pray for good, health, peace of mind, prosperity as though they were in another place, if not in another time—and ignore the good we have.

The object of my personal quest is: *A pattern for living, individually and with others; and personal dignity through consideration, appreciation, and apperception. The integrity of my soul is not of the mind but of the heart, a heartfelt desire to express* *the concrete physical evidence of the ultimate through spiritual living.*

Spiritual integrity transcends words and their meaning. Spiritual integrity is concerned life and living. We live our lives, not daily, not hourly, but each and every moment. The only possibility of irrelevance exists through failure to seek—and thus find—a frame of reference to which I can relate.

YOUR ASSIGNMENT FOR THIS WEEK

Essential to wholeness are questions of essence:

"Am I making an effort to be healthy? Are my attitudes good—or are they devastating to my soul? Do I have a concern that embraces more than just myself? Do I really want what I ask for? Enough to do more than ask?"

The problems religions seek to solve are harsh and bitter. Do any of the following words apply to me—in any way? *Ignorance. Centered in self. Malice. A language of generalities? Do I know that everything is relevant to my well-being? Do I practice what I proclaim? If I am unhealthy in any way need I first be honest with myself?*

Remember—

The first element of wholeness in any area of mind, body, and affairs is acceptance of the reality of the healing presence of God, regardless of the name we give this presence and power.

Out of this acceptance and knowledge proceeds the concept of deeper truth; out of this truth comes understanding.

Out of a world of disillusionment comes reality.

God speaks! If we listen, the answer will be *all that we seek.*

Would you have health? Then you must first be at home in the world of spirit and recognize that *all* is spirit.

"Be thou an example of the believers, in word, in conversation, . . . in faith . . . " —I Timothy 4:12

MAKE THIS—

YOUR DAILY AFFIRMATION FOR THE WEEK:·

I contemplate the healing presence within. I speak calmly, of spirit, knowing that my words are of the spirit. Relaxed, I release, I let go, I know God, and I embrace in mind, body, and affairs only that which is good and of God."

Your basis of reality in daily living

The first element of healing is acceptance of the reality of the healing presence of God. The divinity of man lies not in what he has, but in his potential for expression. In areas of the mind, man can express half-truths and reflect the unreality of a "false god," while he continues to claim that he is created in the image and likeness of God. Through half-truth—visualizing, speaking, or being less than God-like: experiencing disorder in any area of life—we have worshipped false idols. We are guilty of idolatry. *("Idolaters resemble their idols." —Psalm 115:8) And though we are created in the image and likeness of God, we have distorted that likeness.* The "Midrash" of the Hebrews interprets the verse Deuteronomy 1:10, as if enscribed: *"Lo, today you are like the stars in heaven, but in the future you will resemble the Master."*

"I contemplate the healing presence within. I speak calmly, knowing that my words are of the spirit. Relaxed, I release, I let go, I know God, and I embrace in mind, body, and affairs only that which is good and of God"

Your self-development questions

All things have a reason for existing: there is nothing that exists without a reason. The questions which follow will stimulate you into a questing, questioning frame of reference—to better comprehend the world in which you live—*and your very important part in it.*

Question 1. In Matthew 7:24, Jesus said, *"Judge not according to* *the appearance, but judge righteous judgment.''* Often this seems to be easier said than done. *What would be one certain way to always "Judge righteous judgment and not according to the appearance?"*

Question 2. *"My reward is with me, to give every man according as his work shall be." —Revelations 22:12. What does this mean to you?*

Question 3. A consciousness of any law gives us the freedom to obey or disobey that law, but we cannot avoid or circumvent its consequences. *Why do you suppose so many presume to break, flaunt, and dispute the law of mind and spirit, and at the same time decry the results?* There is little doubt that "ignorance of the law" can hardly be the reason, for common sense tells most of us the "Way."

Question 4. One definition of ethics is "accepted rules of conduct." This bespeaks of integrity. The "integrity of life" is deeper than a sense of moral conduct. It must embrace accepted rules of conduct in every area of life, i.e., a consciousness concretely expressed as relevant to the divine. *List definite steps which you will persuade others, by your example to incorporate in their lives.*

> **"See . . . that thou make all things according to the pattern shewed to thee in the mount." —Hebrews 8:5**

"STIMULATORS TO ACTION"—

> *In public speaking one must have something to say,*
> *and speak loudly*
> *enough to be heard, clearly enough to be understood,*
> *honestly enough to be trusted,*
> *and lovingly enough to be one with those who listen.*
> *—A pattern for life?*
> *"Silence"—that link with the source of wisdom—a sound-*
> *less voice within, beyond reason, intellect or understanding.*
> *But to be listened to—heeded—in acceptance or rejection*
> *of ideas, attitudes and actions!*
> *"The word is very nigh unto thee, in thy mouth, and in thy heart,*
> *that thou mayest do it."—Deuteronomy 30:14*
> *"Incline your ear, and come unto me: hear, and your soul shall*
> *live."* —Isaiah 55:3

WEEKLY PROGRAM
NUMBER
14

The Law of Body, Mind and Your Daily Affairs

Whoever you are, wherever you might be, it cannot be denied that whatever your morals, culture, philosophy, hopes, dreams, fears, aspirations, your life is a multi-colored reinforcement of something beyond experience alone. But whatever your experience, life is a passage through time and eternity.

As you pass through time and eternity, there will be moments without form and days without direction, when answers sought will not be found. But there will always be signals to action. At times your life may seem comprehensible and at other times incomprehensible, but there are always words, sounds and signs—principles of faith and postulates of conduct—each saying, *"There is a law, and its demand is absolute."* Though you may passionately disavow relatedness of your consciousness to the theme of your life, the intensification of your experience is—yours?—or mine? And by whom is it made?

If there is a law of mind, body, and affairs, how do we recognize it, apply it, and improve our lives? Perhaps the simplest admonition would be, "Do unto others as ye would have them do unto you." But there is also an admonition of precedence: *"Seek ye first the kingdom of God, and his righteousness, and all these things shall be added unto you." —Matthew 6:33.* The basic concept is considered in the verse that follows: *"Take therefore no thought for the morrow: for the morrow shall take thought for the things of itself."* We need no rationalization to know that we prefer peace of mind, health, and prosperity to that which most of us experience. We have the choice—shall we begin to *"Seek first the kingdom of God"*?

94

Men and women have felt emotion much deeper than they can express. At such moments discourse ends, and something beyond experience begins.

Begin this sense of quiet, contemplative meditation by reading the first seven verses of the twenty-first chapter of the Book of Revelation. As you read, peruse the experience as yours and *experience* the reading. Become acquainted with yourself and with *"The Master."*

Now: Make no attempt toward a transcendence. Muse for more than a moment upon that for which interpretations have been exceedingly varied.

In a relaxed and comfortable position, back straight, hands in lap, sit for several minutes, breathing deeply, holding both inhalation and exhalation. Gradually accept and embrace that revelation from your reading of the Book of Revelation.

Allow this to develop into the rapture of complete and total silence—without sight or sound.

Your experience can and should be beyond common discourse—transcendent reality. You and the thought which has come to you are one for you have gone to it.

Document that which has been revealed to you.

And document your realization of what this means to you.

MAKE THIS—

YOUR DAILY AFFIRMATION FOR THE WEEK:

"This day I do give thanks that there is a quality which transmutes hope into expression, expression into experience, and experience into all that is or ever can be good. This quality is the enablement of man and the intent of God. I give thanks and seek, in every way, to be a valid expression of love."

Your basis of reality in daily living

Though much *is* demanded of me, it is no more than is required of all others. Not a small share of the crucial difference between happiness and sorrow, the imaged and the conceived, meaning and void, the evident and the concealed, that which is required of me in every area of human relations, if relationship is to have meaning with depth, is courtesy, affection, interest, and a willing heart and hand—all a part and portion—*the absolute demand of the law of living.*

The building of a life is as much a work of art as are sculptured portals decorating the aesthetic monument we call a cathedral. Only the tools differ.

"This day I do give thanks that there is a quality which transmutes hope into expression; expression into experience, and experience into all that is or ever can be good. This quality is the potential of man and the intent of God. I give thanks and seek, in every way, to be a valid expression of love."

A life transformed—

Those who live in the present have an eye on the future and are part of an ever young and active world. They do the things others dream of. Theirs is a vision of meaning, participation, growth, accomplishment—*involvement*—with life, with others, with meaning, and with membership in total commitment of the self to the best expression of the self in every area of life.

Your self-development questions

Question 1. It is an established fact that most people proceed from habit, custom, and personal inclination rather than from logic or concern beyond the self. *Assuming that "every human being is seeking the better things of life," how would you relate the importance of spiritual comprehension to an intelligent person who believes in "self sufficiency without the spirit?"*

Question 2. In the Bible, in I Kings 3:5-14, we read: *"... the Lord appeared to Solomon in a dream by night; and God said, 'Ask what I shall give you.' And Solomon said, "Give thy servant ... an understanding mind ..,.. that I may discern between good and evil ..." It pleased the Lord that Solomon had asked this. And God said to him, "Because you have asked this, and have not asked for yourself long life or riches or the life of your enemies, but have asked for yourself understanding to discern what is right, behold, I now do according to your word. Behold, I give you a wise and discerning mind . . . I give you also what you have not asked, both riches and honour . . . And if you will walk in my ways, keeping my statutes and my commandments . . . I will lengthen your days."* For thousands of years philosophers have wrangled with the problem of why men without scruples or conscience succeed while good men of equal ability fail. *How would your understanding reduce this equitably to the teachings of religionists and that which we see in the world around us?*

Question 3. It has been said, and no doubt you will agree, that honesty is the best policy. Most of us are far from guileless in the art of falsification to self and others. Honesty IS the best policy. However, honesty with the self demands the discipline of facing facts. Honesty with others makes of us denizens demurring to tell the truth. *Now, if man's intellectual and spiritual resources are drawn upon, precisely how will one be completely honest with oneself and others, and how can one avoid unpleasant and sometimes unacceptable reactions?*

Question 4. Most individuals do not care whether contemporary science or philosophy support or oppose the dogma of their religion. If his belief is absurd or unreasonable, too often the individual doubles his commitment to it. *How can you and I know we are not guilty of this same tendency?*

"It is the Spirit that beareth witness, because the Spirit is truth." —I John 5:6

"STIMULATORS TO ACTION"—

Look upon and give thought to a little child.
There is much of interest and wonder that bestirs
his mind through the world in which he lives.
In looking upon this small degree of thee
and me, our perspective is a wide horizon.
We know the potential which lies within.

The interest and wonder of the offspring of man

produces the well-spring of God.
As the child, take an interest in the world
around you—be not merely an observer.
You will participate.

"Do you need proof of God? Does one light a torch to see the sun?"

—Oriental Wisdom

How to Live in the "Now"

It is not without reason that man demands a purpose beyond existence. Throughout his history, he has written volumes seeking to elevate his mind above his affairs. There is no doubt that he is intelligent, rational, striving, and struggling. Yet with the tremendous power of his intellect it is not unreasonable to ask, "Why, with a mind surpassing the world in which he finds himself, does he find himself in a world no better than that which he has made?"

He believes in others and in things. A delusive mirage obscures him from himself. He doubts. And all the while the reality he seeks is the reality he is, if he would cease the struggle, desist from striving, and put into practice the power of mind that is his.

He believes there is within him potential beyond expression. *There is within him power beyond whatever he has expressed.* But how necessary it is for him—*for you and me*—to stop reaching out to another time, another place, or another person—and relate to the time in which we find ourselves, to those with whom we are priviledged to be, in this present place.

We supposedly have an interest in the highest of aims. How strong is our faith in the spirit leading us toward the ideal and the end? We demand a reason for being: We have this right. But with every right there is responsibility. We have the responsibility to organize our mind, body, and affairs according to spirit if we expect anything from spirit.

Part of this organizational responsibility lies in knowing that spirit is always present and in the present. As deeply as we seek that which we seek, we must know, determine, and proceed, not some time in the future, or for that which we would have in the future, but now. In lieu of the future, we must live, think, act, do, and be—*here and now—in the present and in the presence of God.*

YOUR ASSIGNMENT FOR THIS WEEK

An aching heart does not need solace in the future, but now. A plant grows only in the present. An individual evolves only when he recognizes that the only time he ever has is the present, and lives accordingly.

Resolve: To make the most and the very best of each moment and of every circumstance—now.

Do you have a higher aim? If you do, defy every thing that would keep you from that aim.

Realize: The present is the only time you will ever have. Intellectual defiance will blind that divinity unalterably in all that you encounter as well as in that which you seek.

In the total human experience you are not the whole. But you are a very important part of every experience. And you are part of that experience now.

Put down on a separate sheet the ways in which you can relate—now—to that which heretofore you may not have admitted relationship.

MAKE THIS—

YOUR DAILY AFFIRMATION FOR THE WEEK:

"There is much that I would do. There is one thing that I can do. I can set a goal, make a resolution, and be consistent daily in reminding myself of that goal or resolution. Then I am receptive to the means of fulfillment of my goal."

Your basis of reality in daily living

Whatever you or I would have come to pass, we must give thought to. And the consideration must be constant—we must hold to that which we would have for more than a moment. The individual who carries this quest for more than the moment discovers a new awareness and possesses a future without the need of planning for it. It will come in spite of appearances or seeming obstacles.

Living in the present, his image extends to the world in which he lives. Here he finds causes, results, and rewards. As he holds to that which he would have, he is in context with more than time. He is contiguous with reality and adjacent to his goal.

Your self-development questions

Question 1. In *The Spiritual Crisis of Man,* Paul Brunton said, "... salvation lies not only in the timed future but also in the timeless Now—which is not the same as the timeful present." *What does and could this mean to you?*

Question 2. Visual images appear within the minds of most people. Most of these images are of that which they would like to have now, but the image is held apart as something that will possibly come in the future. *When we have the power to create images, why do most of us hold to the image in another period of time rather than in the present?*

Question 3. Quoting Mr. Brunton again: "No one can measure the infinite power and no one can weigh it. No one can touch it with his hands or see it with his eyes. Yet something that emanates from it mysteriously takes form in and as our experience." *In a very real sense, what are we talking about, and can you phrase it so that others will comprehend what is being said?*

Question 4. Truth, as most of us live, know and, experience it, is but a whisper of a roaring sound. God is interwoven inextricably with man and all he will ever experience. Yet man denies himself by the very process by which he can know God, Truth, and himself. *What can you do to extricate yourself from this form of Spiritual delusion?*

"Now we see through a glass, darkly; but then face to face: Now I know in part; but then shall I know even as Also I am known."
                                        —I Corinthians 13:12

—All things are yours." —I Corinthians 3:21

How a man learned that failure
can be turned into success

Some people learn with a sense of shock that what they would have out of life they could have had long before the moment of realization.

Not too long ago such a man came to see me. In our discussion of his problem (which was that little or nothing productive ever seemed to happen in his life), I soon discovered that what he desired, he did nothing about. He told me that he had read a number of books on "How To Be a Success," "I've Made Mine—You Can Make Yours," "Millionaires Overnight," "Health and Healing Without Medication," "Friends for the Asking," but the results were hardly productive.

As we discussed the principles in the book, a light suddenly shone in his face. He told me again of the books he had read. Somehow he just hadn't realized that now was the only time, and if he was going to accomplish anything, he would have to begin by doing something, and doing it NOW! What he had learned is that we can read, discuss, and contemplate the many and varied paths to something better, but that *one must do something with that which has been given.* I shared with him several chapters of this book, which was then in manuscript form. He has failed in several things since our time together in discussion. However he learned an important rule of life and success. That *failure isn't the end of the world.* He also learned that what he put his faith and action into became the cornerstone of that which he succeeded in building. And—he built a great new life for himself, not only in business success, but in his family and social life as well.

"STIMULATORS TO ACTION"–

Give thought to this:
Man is like and may be likened to a tree.
Of all the untold millions of trees
every one is rooted in the self-same earth. Man, you and I,
are rooted in soil of spirit. As the tree draws what it is
from the soil in which it grows—you and I have ever
available to us all that would ever nourish, sustain, support,
and develop us.

How to Build the Cornerstone of Your New Life

In what do you place your faith? On what do you build your life? Does your opinion of yourself give credence and credit to your relationship with something beyond yourself? Or is it a vivid expression of nothing? Poverty, lack, illness, unhappiness, and inability to relate to others, conditions, and circumstances are not conditions to which we have been subjected. These are evidence of deception of the self, occasionally unconscious but more often through lack of dedication to a purpose. Upon purpose, design, goal, the "inner spirit of God" (by whatever name we call God), we build the cornerstone of successful living, precious health, true prosperity, the verity of truth, and a very real object of knowledge—peace of mind.

Discovery—or disenchantment? All life, every condition, each individual is in a state of constant change. Nothing is in a state of static constancy. Life, man—even nations—discover, determine, and evolve, or they regress.

A very great educator made a wise observation: "All people do not want to be educated. Many resist education all their lives." Thus education and the impetus to an improved, constructive, and creative life " . . . becomes a burden." —Gilbert Highet, "Man's Unconquerable Mind," p.75. So the first aspect of a better life is the consideration, *"Am I willing to learn? Do I have the desire to really change my life and affairs for the better?"* A second consideration is an awareness that whatever I encounter, if I fail to contribute to it in a positive sense, I negate that very same thing. This relates to health of the body, peace of mind, conditions of

103

my affairs, and all that my world encompasses." How truly it was said by him who wrote so long ago: *"The heart of him that hath understanding seeketh knowledge." —Proverbs 15:14*

Let it not be said of thee:

"Thou has left behind
Powers that will work for thee; air, earth, and skies;
There's not a breathing of the common wind
   That will forget thee; thou has great allies;
Thy friends are exultations, agonies,
   And love, and man's unconquerable mind."

"Thou has left behind—
Powers that will work for thee . . . "
                         —Wordsworth, "To Toussaint L'Ouverture"

The cornerstone of life is the embracing, the drawing to and opening of, all worthy of life; the releasing of self-indulgence to anything that is not larger than life itself.

Thoughts are never wasted. Give thought to this! *Good or bad—thoughts are never wasted.* It is only life, opportunity, development, and meaning that are uninhabited, unproductive, rejected, unused, squandered, or thrown away. Have you decided yet *HOW GREAT IS THY POSSESSION?*

Embrace this truth: *"I can do all things through Christ (the potential perfection within) which strengtheneth me." —Philippians 4:13.*

YOUR ASSIGNMENT FOR THIS WEEK

This lesson, while brief, demands a profound change of thinking. Reason demands while faith extends beyond the visible to that which can be made visible. Extend your vision beyond your present condition of health or affairs. What would you have in your life which presently you do not?

Know: (and this is the challenge) *"I can do all things through Christ which strengtheneth me."* Know and accept this. Affirm it daily every day this week. And read the selection of your choice, a chapter or a book, on the life of any of our great spiritual precursors. As you seek, that which you seek will seek you out.

The first step in the right direction toward a better life is a good impression of yourself, a good opinion of your fellow man, and the faith in God to prove both impression and opinion.

MAKE THIS—

YOUR DAILY AFFIRMATION FOR THE WEEK:

"I live in a very real world: even that which appears to be purely of the mind or the imagination has reality to it, because of its existence within my mind. Upon the thoughts within my mind I determine all that transpires. Therefore, my thoughts being the cornerstone of my life, I choose positive, productive, spiritual, God-oriented thoughts."

Your basis of reality
in daily living

Two things propound a difficult problem for every individual, whether seeking sincerely to make for himself a better life, or merely wishing for one. Intelligent living, the cornerstone of a meaningful life, has an apt comparison in the art and eloquence of public speaking. Mere speech is not art. *Living* implies something beyond existence. To live, really live, one must build on a sound principle, making this principle the very cornerstone of life. Art in life or in speaking requires adherence to a set of rules to be practiced and applied. "Eloquence," in life or in public speaking, reflects the vividness and the solidarity upon which each has been structured.

"I live in a very real world. Therefore the thoughts which are the cornerstone of my life are positive, productive, spiritual, God-oriented thoughts!"

Example. In the lives of men and women around us we have the use and force of good and bad example. Needless to say, their lives and their examples, speak for themselves.

Your self-development questions

Question 1. We are told that to have a better opinion of ourselves, we must think in a more constructive manner regarding ourselves. "Thinking" is defined as: "thought, belief, or opinion, forming a mental image or concept; to meditate upon, to have expectation, or show consideration." *All of us think!* And now the question: *What constructive and objective thought do you have regarding personal growth and your ability to serve the needs of persons other than yourself, i.e., family, friends, church, employer, employees?*

Question 2. All of us like luxury. One luxury we can ill afford is the luxury of self-satisfaction, nor can we afford the luxury and visitation of any thought that fails to bring forth potential. Determining to have organized and orderly thinking will result in a sense of purpose and an absolute assurance of the results. *What will you add to this that will not only make your life richer but also more abundant for an increasing number of people?*

Question 3. Nature always aims at perfection. That which does not grow and evolve falls by the wayside. This is Nature's way of insuring that life shall not only continue but be abundant. There is no difference between this and human life. *List several factors of motivation that would stimulate others, and you, to an action of growth and evolvement.*

Question 4. Philosophy, unlike mathematics, does not have the requisite of scientific evidence. No special observations or experiments necessitate positive conclusion. Self-evident principles prove conclusions and solve problems for the philosopher and the mathematician. *Theologically, an article of faith must extend beyond assumption. How do we remove ourselves from the "vacuum" of dependency upon faith without proof and assumption without results?*

"I will instruct thee and teach thee in the way which thou shalt go." —Psalm 32:8

"STIMULATORS TO ACTION"—

If we were to turn to God, asking, "What are our greatest assets?" we might be inspired to know

that the answer is: "Your mind, your body, and your spirit!"
While we know this, we also know this is but part of
the answer; for the spirit within proclaims that we can do,
be, and express more than we have done, been, or expressed,
while all the time revealing the way—if we but listen.

You would be moved? You would be stimulated to action?
Recall the admonition, "I can do all things through Christ
(the potential perfection within) which strengtheneth me."
                                    —Philippians 4:13

WEEKLY PROGRAM NUMBER
17

The Value of Prayer

While it may appear that we pray for any of a thousand reasons, we really pray for only two reasons: To change an undesirable, unwanted, unpleasant condition, or to acquaint ourselves with God. If we pray for the first reason, we err, for to know God is to benefit by directive prayer. Prayer to change circumstances, conditions, or people will be answered, but not in the manner of expectation. We are praying to a lesser power than God—to them or to ourselves. We are holding to an image, a concept of that which we would no longer have rather than reaching out toward that which would be ours through spiritual understanding. We don't "get rid of" anything. We replace old conditions, ideas, and experiences, with new, vital, life-giving direction *through directive prayer*. So long as we demand the sacrifice of others, and the riddance of those things of which we do not approve, our prayer is answered in disapproval and dissatisfaction of self.

Every man desires freedom: freedom to go his own way, progress, stagnate, and determine for himself and others what life should be according to *his* standards. To be socially consistent is to be prayerfully constant. What am I saying? We cannot limit nor extend our range of good until that which we would have for ourselves, we would also have for others. Love cannot be extended except through an extension of love. Understanding cannot be accepted until it is given. No matter how dispassionate I may be, I must be passionate in what I would seek for myself in that I would also seek the same for all others. If I would pray to know God, I must know what prayer is. Knowing God, I know what prayer is. Knowing God, I know my fellow man: I am in prayer.

In the thousands of books on prayer, almost without exception, one is struck by the volumes on the reasons for prayer—*and the paucity of expression of what prayer is.* A rendering of meaning, though one man's definition of prayer, is worthy of iteration:

"ONE MAN'S DEFINITION OF PRAYER"

An effort of man to communicate with God whom man considers to be beyond view and vision; a bringing into perspective, a relationship with God and fellow man, all and everything he can see, feel, touch—the very air he breathes—for prayer is God! And God is all!

YOUR ASSIGNMENT FOR THIS WEEK

Can you grasp the meaning in terms of loftier values than that which appearance and experience may have revealed?

While we realize that we are constrained by the mind to think as men have thought, we can know, beyond the limitation of mind alone, that "we expand our vision" as we "extend" our vision. Prayerfully consider "one man's definition of prayer."

Write the many implications it will have on your life through its new perspective.

Read these, your new understanding perceptions, each day this coming week.

At the end of the week record the differences you have experienced because of the revealing of that which was obscured.

Scripture: To be read daily: The epistle of Paul to Philemon. (This, though one of the shortest books of the Bible, can be one of the most meaningful to you).

A thought to ponder: We seek answers to questions. There are no answers *unless* we seek. We strive to find meaning. There is no meaning unless we contribute meaning. We long for importance. For us, there is no importance until we recognize how important everyone and everything else is to us. We would know peace of mind, prosperity and health. They will elude us *until ... Do you not know the answer?*

"Order my steps in thy word." —Psalm 119:133

MAKE THIS—

YOUR DAILY AFFIRMATION FOR THE WEEK:

"Consideration is the substance of truth and the meaning of prayer. I am considerate in all I do."

The basis of reality
in daily living

If I am to know the substance of truth and the meaning of prayer, I must know the meaning of consideration. To be considerate is to be gentle, loving, understanding, giving, sharing, and able to receive. But consideration is more: it is to be a successful human being—successful through spiritual awareness. *"I am kind, I am gentle, I am considerate in all I do."* To be considerate is strength, for a considerate person is strong in the Lord *(the law of his own being)*. To be considerate is to be a blessing and to be blessed. To be considerate is to be prayerful. *The very nature of all we seek may be found in the simple word—"consideration."*

"Consideration is the substance of truth and the meaning of prayer. I am considerate in all I do."

"Teach me thy way, O Lord, that I may walk in thy truth."
                                                              —Psalm 86:11

What will you do?

As you seek health, peace of mind, prosperity, success—a better and more meaningful way of life—it is important that you recognize that much is demanded of you. You must believe as an absolute, unchanging fact that whatever you want, *you must do something about,* in a positive, assured acceptance that principles, teachings, and guidance are *valid only when applied. WHAT WILL YOU DO?*

Your self-development questions

Question 1. For some a church is a place of worship, renewal, uplifting, and unfolding of spiritual qualities from within. *What do YOU expect from your church? Your minister? What do you believe your church and your minister have the right to expect from you?*

Question 2. As one goes to church to receive, so also one must be receptive to receive. To receive anything, one must also give. *What are you giving to your church, the source of your good?*

Question 3. Words are symbols of thought. Words also are the verbal expression of an idea. Action is the emotional and intellectual involvement beyond words. Interest motivates us beyond thought and word. Words are symbols of thought! *Prescribe for yourself several ways in which you can discipline your activities to make life more meaningful.*

Question 4. *"I'm doing the best I can,"* is an overrated and under-productive statement. In retrospect, all of us can determine where we might have done things differently or better. Akin to the old saying *practice makes perfect–* only correct practice leads to perfection. To assist yourself in doing the best you can, ask yourself, "Am I doing the best I can? Am I really doing the very best I can?" *Summarize your thoughts about these questions—remembering there is no excuse and little defense for most of the answers we might contrive.*

"By their fruits ye shall know them." –Matthew 7:20

"STIMULATORS TO ACTION"–

The way to begin is to commence!
Drop whatever you are doing and do whatever you
are dropping. Lay aside that which burdens. Grasp
tightly that which uplifts. "Be strong in the Lord"
(The law of your own being).

"A doer of the work . . . shall be blessed in his deed."
–James 1:25

"The purpose of prayer"

Our understanding of religion, philosophy, activity of every kind—everything—is structured around the framework of words. We recognize words as language, though we may or may not comprehend the language. The average individual experiences limitation, not by the paucity of language, but by unfamiliarity with it. He recognizes a tree, a stone, or a rock, but he rarely knows the composition of the tree, the life and history of the times in which it lived, each season, wet or dry, abundant, or barren—all recognizable in the shape and width of each ring. Wind and storm are depicted as twist and turn and each tree tells a thousand things in the universal language of nature. Too many men think a tree is but a tree. A rock or a stone tell of more than earthly mineral matter. Each rock and stone and everything else has carried with it tales of other times, of animals, trees, land, sea and mountains moved. Each is conversant in a language beyond the barrier of names and titles and words.

In the language we use and fail to comprehend is the history, the power, and the purpose of what we are and what we might be. *What are we? Sound? Substance?* Words are more than words, names, or titles: they are the language, the life, and the meaning we give them. As time and history and events have left their mark upon rock, rill, stone, and tree, we are the meaning we have given to the words we use. One unfamiliar with the universal language of nature hears a different sound and experiences a different meaning. To one unfamiliar with the universal language of life specifically the spiritual Life, there is little more meaning than a rock, a stone, or just a tree. In the language of spirit, of church, of philosophy, and of life, there is much that is metaphysical and mysterious. And we are not mystics. We are confused by the language we use. We know the purpose of a church and of going to church, but we take little with us for having been in church. We speak of prayer and we know neither prayer or its purpose. Prayer, directed prayer, as the rock or the tree, has a universal language, understandable by all—*if any would understand.* Directed prayer is much more than a word; it is purpose! And the purpose of prayer is effective, dynamic meaning in your life. But there can be little meaning in our lives unless the language we use comprehends the purpose of every man's prayer.

What is the purpose of prayer? *It is meaning!* This meaning that may be likened to a vast reservoir. There is immense power in water thus gathered. In its most minimal use we may look upon it and know it to be there. We can see it as a thing of beauty and find quiet renewal and respite within our soul. Or we may decide to venture forth and let it support us above its mirrored surface. Again, we may step in and experience the refreshing contact that only immersion will give. We may even, in a moment of disregard for the self, swallow a little of this water. *Now!* we have experienced the purpose of the reservoir.

To make useful the purpose of the reservoir, preparation had to be made: it must be dammed so that the water can collect. This required concrete and steel. To be able to "draw" upon the purpose of prayer requires a damming up, a shutting out, a keeping in, of certain ideas, thoughts, words, and concepts. The purpose of a dam is to control water. Prayer also had the purpose of a "gathering in," the ability to control, direct, and channel thought. As with the reservoir, preliminary preparation is required. We must prepare if there is to be a purpose in prayer. This preparation is *concentration,* the bulwark, *meditation.* Our completed reservoir is *"the Silence."*

Join with me in experiencing that which we have built. We are all concentrating upon something. For this moment let us be selective. Now we know what we would have. Presently, we will not concentrate on this. Rather we will seek an influx of spirit. Close your eyes. Imagine a flowing stream of water. Bending low (within your mind), dip your hand into this living stream. It is refreshing. With anticipatory vision, feel, as with water, this substance encompassing your body. Then create a mental image of your body, with every cell separate, and this flowing stream surrounding each cell—*penetrating, permeating, becoming one. Now, this living stream and you are one. There is healing and wholeness in this. Your mind and body are at peace. Your mind, your body, and your affairs are now encompassed completely and totally—and in order. Wholeness! Let these words ring out the power and the purpose of prayer.*

We live by more than words

We live by more than words. We live by the purpose of our prayer. The lines in your face, the elements of your life, show the language of the purpose of your prayer. For this coming week devote twenty minutes each day entering the stream of spirit. Your life will show purpose to your prayer.

WEEKLY PROGRAM
NUMBER
18

The Purpose of Prayer

Not even the briefest consideration of prayer can have meaning without concern for attitudes of mind. Failing in this, there is no understanding of prayer, its meaning, purpose, results, and consequences.

Superficially, the monk in the monastary and the man in the Mafia would appear farther apart than distant galaxies— *yet both pray* and both receive answers to their prayer. The one, by intent, seeks God and meaning and fellow man. The other is concerned with self and motivated deeply by the self, and acquires that which makes others question, "Why and how?" *Yet both pray.*

One looks upon the face of all, and all is beautiful, good, and divine. Rich and abundant is his peace. The other looks upon life and knows that all is his and the means by which he attains his goals becomes an epithet. He knows no peace. *Both men are deep in prayer.*

Vocabulary, concern, interest, intent, purpose, philosophy, truth, and logic differ. Both relate to God and man—one blindly; the other, knowingly. Both pray. A universe apart! A moral enmity! One, libation and abnegation, profaning purpose. The other? Selfless—giving, sharing, being—inheritor of mind, spirit, power and purpose—dignifying the incidence of his presence. In both an attitude of mind! For, prayer is an attitude of mind. The purpose of your prayer? Consider:

Despite differences, each involves the other. When you and I cease to be oriented purely by the self, the purpose of our prayer will construct the whole philosophy of a way of life. Prayer, then,

115

creates beyond the incidental and emotional. It is the incidence of ideas analogous to more, much more than a meaningful moment and a thing of the moment.

YOUR ASSIGNMENT FOR THIS WEEK

Out of your daily experience, search for means to have your life represent a new spiritual quality in relation to others.

Specifically: Become still in mind and body. Enter this period of quiet with this thought: *"I am receptive to divine spirit. I allow nothing to enter my mind or affairs other than that which is God-like."* This requires a discipline of thought for all is God-like though we may not observe its God-like qualites.

This week: To vary the means of transformation, read one of the great philosophers, visit an art gallery, spend an hour with a book of poetry, attend a musical.

And: Select a portion of your Bible to read each day—*with another.*

Inscribe within your notebook the differences you detect within yourself. Spend an hour in quiet contemplation of *who you are,* and *where—and why.*

"Comparing spiritual things with spiritual." —Corinthians 2:13

MAKE THIS—

YOUR DAILY AFFIRMATION FOR THE WEEK:

"Henceforth I begin each day in prayer—with purpose. A positive, dynamic change of self is the result of prayer."

Your basis of reality in daily living

Directive or correct prayer is an end in itself. It is correct thinking, an attitude and posture of mind, proof evident of positive, effective, spiritually oriented results.

What I experience as the result of prayer is profound considera-tion of what I think, feel, and am—a direct result of that reflected upon and contemplated. The consequence or reward is only that to which I have given consent.

The agonies, joys, and a thousand images—all the prayers we have prayed!

Transmuted thought and the imaged concept become mirrored as experience. We *conceive* and fail to *know* that we produce the only answer to every prayer. There is but one purpose to prayer: correct thinking, an attitude and posture of mind, proof evident of positive, effective, spiritually oriented results. Anything less is prayer which lacks the magnitude of chosen results.

"Henceforth I begin each day in prayer—with purpose. A positive, dynamic change of self is the result of prayer."

A point worth restating—

Every human being is seeking the better things of life. How diligently he pursues that which he seeks, is the determinant of his success or failure. The material which follows each discipline is a positive guideline in that search. While it is important to answer all the questions, there are no right or wrong answers in terminology. However, there are right answers both in understanding and in application. Answer briefly and in the light of how you feel regarding the questions. But for your own evolvement, do answer the questions. This can be done in a notebook and kept for future reference and reconsideration.

Your self-development questions

Question 1. The characters in a novel may have a reality beyond reality. Life is the great reality. So that you may not only live realistically, but powerfully, dynamically, spiritually, and meaningfully, set down in your notebook a word for each day of the week that you will incorporate as an action for that day.

Question 2. This is but a start. *Outline the first of what will be a permanent, daily draft of inspirational ideas, evolving concepts, and considerations producing positive and desirable results in your* *life. Note: After this beginning, I suggest a small notebook which can be carried with you, for this purpose.*

Question 3. We need to find ways to relate to everything. In simple terms state *how you will relate to:* Church; an unpleasant alcoholic; an unfriendly person; to music you do not understand; to God.

Question 4. Life is both abstract and concrete. Realities such as earning a living, getting along with others, or ill health, all appear as realities, yet each is abstract because each involves emotion, intellect, and change. *Outline a formula for concrete living and then a formula to establish effective living.*

"Whosoever will be great among you, let him be your minister."
                                              —Matthew 20:26

"STIMULATORS TO ACTION"—

*Know this: You are a son of God with great potential
    and a divine inheritance.
        Proclaim aloud, "I am a son of God! I have great
    potential! All the ends of the earth are mine!"
    "I am imbued with the spirit that sets me free,
        develops potential, and produces results. Richness
    of life is mine!" Affirm! Proclaim! Believe!
        Accept! Embrace! Receive!*

WEEKLY PROGRAM
NUMBER

19

What Prayer Can Do for You

If prayer is anything at all, it must be something that does something, changes something, or benefits someone.

Prayer is an attitude of mind, and an execution of thought. It is what we think. For some, it may be well for them to bare their souls and say what others and they know about themselves: *"Lord, I've been a lying, cheating, thieving, sinful individual. Perhaps my lying, cheating, and thieving, has robbed and taken most from me—but what I don't have, I guess I can't share with others. In that way, maybe I also take from them. If the power of prayer is thinking of and turning to you, Lord I've got part of the praying done, for I've been doing a lot of thinking. In my sinning, perhaps it's mostly not having done my best. So now, Lord, I turn to the other part—to you—to help me to cleanse my thinking, purify my mind and show me how to apply myself."*

The foregoing may not apply to you. If it does, talking it out will be good for your soul, will change your thinking, and will change you.

An interesting consideration we must make regarding the power of prayer concerns an understanding of God. I would proclaim that the power of prayer is an understanding of God. *And an understanding of God is a workable relatedness to all things. If you accept this, know that* there is much man wants and thinks he prays for. He wants God to do away with war, alleviate suffering, change the world, and stop the rain. In the life of man, God does nothing without man; *except that you and I know that the power of prayer must be an idea in our minds which we utilize to do something about that which must be done.*

119

YOUR ASSIGNMENT FOR THIS WEEK

Reflect upon the following:

It has been said that, "If man were not here to observe the earth and all upon it, these things, in actuality, would not exist." For him they would not exist. However, man is here and all he beholds and is willing to discern does exist whether he doubts, believes, or disbelieves.

Now: Reducing very real and lofty principles to the simplest terminology, equate the outer world with your inner world. A tree, a mountain, the desert, or a sea are all to be gazed upon, taken in and received—to become part of our inner world and our oral relation as we seek to share what we have seen. This is also true of clouds, colors, and moments of inspiration. But that which inspires—a word, a kindness, an understanding—is *not to be looked upon, but sensed and felt.*

There is a greatness to your inner world because it can neither be seen nor touched. This is that subtle something I choose to call *the power of prayer.* It has a seductive quality for those who choose to look within. *Look within all others first.* This will fill you with love and kindness, compassion, and understanding—for what you seek, you find among the seeking: a very real world when the bystander becomes beholden to the world in which he would live. *This is the power of prayer. Go forth in faith and let not this be said of you:*

"Except ye see signs and wonder, ye will not believe." —John 4:48

Select an assignment of your own choice (but do select an assignment). Be as diligent with this as you would with an assignment given to you. Write it down.

"This is the covenant that I will make, . . . I will put my laws into their mind, and write them in their hearts: and I will be to them a God . . . " —Hebrews 8:10

"I shall be satisfied, when I awake, with thy likeness." —Psalm 17:15

MAKE THIS—

YOUR DAILY AFFIRMATION FOR THE WEEK:

"Prayer is one thing: communion between God and man. I pray powerfully through love and kindness, consideration and under-standing. This day I take a further step. With precision, I direct my destiny through ease of quietude, mindful that the power of prayer is a great force, but is in itself a power without stress."

Your basis of reality
in daily living

In the revelation of God in your life and mine, it becomes important to distinguish between power and force. Force produces an effect by effort or exertion, constraining one to an unnatural posture or bearing. Power is the ability to dispense with force, allowing the path of least resistance to occasion the desired results. The power of prayer is the validity of faith, bearing fruit of spiritual attunement. *"This day I direct my destiny through love and kindness, consideration and understanding."*

"The people that do know their God shall be strong." —Daniel 11:32

"In all . . . things we are more than conquerors through him."
                                                        —Romans 8:37

Success in that which you would do: *"The Harvest of an Idea"* Our problem? *We don't persist in and sustain a good idea, a workable plan,* until it (the plan) bears fruit. Realize that every moment and every situation presents opportunities for immature or mature actions, attitudes, and judgments.

Your self-development questions

Question 1. Much is said about changes necessary to make this a better world. On occasion we hear the statement, "Why doesn't

God do something about it?" A better question would be, "What does God (or something within me) expect me to do about making the world better? What can I do that I am not doing?" *Write your answers to these two questions.*

Question 2. We have some of the most inspiring books in the world in the books of the Bible. *List some of the books of the Bible which were inspiring to you, stating exactly what the inspiration was. If you are unable to recall any which inspired you, read at random and when inspired, write down the inspiration and how it can and will relate to your daily life.*

Question 3. While we read many inspiring thoughts, statements, and admonitions in the Bible, we also read statements such as: *"Vengeance is mine, saith the Lord." Or "A readiness to revenge all disobedience."* This latter passage is from II Corinthians 10:6, the former is from the book of Romans. A reading of the book of Romans, Chapter 12, will clear away the veil of misunderstanding. *Before reading this chapter, write down what these scriptures appear to mean.*

Question 4. Every church, temple, and synagogue is attempting to serve the needs of those who seek. *So that you can clearly know what it is you seek, and in the seeking be helpful to your rabbi, priest, or minister, arrange in order of importance the following as you would have them presented to you—1. A healing ministry. 2. General and varied topics. 3. A series of specific lessons. 4. Pertinent issues of the day (this is an area the clergyman is qualified to discuss but often criticized for mentioning). 5. A prayer ministry. 6. Other? Now: why have you selected the first two?*

"He that searcheth the hearts knoweth what is the mind of the Spirit." —Romans 8:27

"STIMULATORS TO ACTION"—

L.W. de Laurence, in The Master Key, stated,
"A crowd is a collective mind, and when you are a member
of a crowd
you are a different man . . . you act like a different man."

Also aptly stated was the observation that "One with God is a majority."

Starting now, as you read this, affirm, proclaim, and assert, "I take God into my life this moment. As a member of this majority I am a different person! I act like a different person! Repeat this: it will stimulate, awaken, animate, encourage, and prompt you to the magnitude of the spirit you are!
"One Lord, one faith, one baptism, One God and Father of all who is above all, and through all, and in you all." —Ephesians 4:5,6.

WEEKLY PROGRAM

NUMBER

20

The Means to Determine the Ends

In each of these programs you are presented with a logical argument designed to give you an understanding of the power of prayer. There *is* an equity between what one prays for and what one receives. However, there too often appears to be an inequity. We focus our attention upon 'what we want and, again, too often seem not to receive that which we have sought. There is an imbalance. *By what means have we endeavored to find the answer to our prayer?*

The faculty of vision, visual perception, deceives the seeker, obscures what he seeks, and again, seems to withhold the petitioned. Are we giving all our attention, belief, hope, faith, and trust to that which we claim we would have? Or are the moments of our search mere moments of seeking with a thousand other things entering our minds and activities and interfering with them?

By what means do we achieve? The answer is a question: *"How much do we want what we want? The answer to the prayer of our seeking is in the effort we consciously, quiescently, vibrantly, dynamically, constantly direct toward the answer.*

The means determine the end! Absolutely nothing exists that will not further our quest. There is no situation, circumstance, person, place, or condition that will keep our good from us *if we are spiritually oriented toward whoever the person may be, whatever the condition, circumstance, or place. But we must see the quality of Christ, God, spirit, and good in this person, condition, circumstance, or place.* This we must do, for it is there and it can be seen if we so much as make the slightest attempt to

124

look beyond the surface *and judge not according to appearance.* With this understanding, whatever the method, the means determine the end. How beautifully and simply it was said in the Book of Job: *"There is a spirit in man: and the inspiration of the Almighty giveth them understanding."* —*Job 32:8.* There is a spirit in man and this *spirit* expresses as all that is beyond the self. These are words and words only *if* we read them, hear them, and speak them, but do not let them affect us. It is then that the *effect* on others is less.

YOUR ASSIGNMENT FOR THIS WEEK

Because of the variety and flexibility of our minds, endless possibilities exist for expression, expansion, and unfoldment. The range beyond the words we read must be the ideas which become eloquent in daily living. The poetry of the mind is like a structure built to house wares. The construction can be of any size, shape, or material—and still be an eyesore. But the building, like poetry of mind and soul, can be functional and beautiful. The words you read must be more than read! They must translate into that which is functional in your life and beyond the intellect—beauty in your living.

Now: This is a long assignment, but it is well worth the reading. Over a period of a week it should prove a rich reward in understanding.

Read: Chapter 32 through to the end of the Book of Job. (It would be a veritable inheritance should you desire to read the entire book).

Meditate upon what you have read. Preface each reading with a time of quiet contemplation.

Daily, after your reading, put down in your words what you have gained in the reading of the particular scripture.

It is not enough to read, write, and feel inspired. Achievement, fulfillment and consumation, must follow. *This will happen if you look for ways to confirm what the words infer.*

"There is a spirit in man: and the inspiration of the Almighty giveth them understanding."

"Search me, O God, and know my heart: try me, and know my thoughts." —Psalm 139:23

MAKE THIS—

YOUR DAILY AFFIRMATION FOR THE WEEK:

"It matters not how I pray, what I say or do—so long as each thought and action has in it the spirit of God." ("I lived as though there were none but He and I in this world." —Brother Lawrence.)"In all thy ways acknowledge Him." —Proverbs 3:6.

Your basis of reality in daily living

This is cause for serious consideration. We may know far too little to articulate the myriad inconsistent images, and agonies which led to any unfilled moment in our life. *We CAN know the manner, the means, and the way to richness and fullness of life.*

The basic ingredient is God. Of course, we find Him in, through, and where we seek. But if we decide to *know* that God *is* in every element representative of the world in which we live, *we will know God in every element in which we live.*

Look for God in everything. Be passionate, like the artist, the poet, or the man who lives beyond himself, and then—*"It matters not how I pray, what I say or do—each thought and action has the spirit of God in it!"*

"Thine ears shall hear a word behind thee, saying, This is the way, walk ye in it, when ye turn to the right hand, and when ye turn to the left." —Isaiah 30:21.

Prelude to the discipline which follows—

Just as the bird, with sound, attracts his own kind—we, with the right or wrong sound attract our own kindred spirits.

Your self-development questions

Question 1. Happiness is a word that is all too often only an articulated sound—a thing of the moment. *Without looking up the definition of happiness, write down what you think it is.*

Question 2. Now that you have committed yourself with your answer, right or wrong, refer to the dictionary definition. *List definitive ways in which you can know, give, and experience happiness, which you might not have been aware of before.*

Question 3. To live beyond narrow confines one must extend the periphery of life. *Observing the most familiar objects, write down (after closer observation) the qualities of beauty you may have missed. Do this with someone you think you really know.*

> **"My convenant will I not break, nor alter the thing that is gone out of my lips."**   —Psalm 89:34

"STIMULATORS TO ACTION"—

The sound of music is an emotion to stir the soul! Yet each note by itself signifies little.

There is the subtle sound: music of mind and spirit.
But we must strike the chord, orchestrate the symphony,
and listen!
Listen when inclined to sound the anvil note upon another's ear.
Listen! Your friend may not say a word, but the voice you
hear will be
"the Silent Sound of God!" Listen! Listen! Listen!

"Keep thy heart with all diligence;
for out of it are the issues of life." —Proverbs 4:23

"There is no speech nor language,
where their voice is not heard." —Psalm 19:3

21

The Hidden Powers Within You

A number of people consider life a challenge. They rise and fall and rise again with the tide and current of adversity. They know, at times, that life and all its ramifications can cause them to call upon resources they may not have known they had. A few individuals not only consider life a challenge *but a marvelous opportunity*. They always attempt, no matter what the experience, to see good in every situation and opportunity in every challenge. And often, though life may not improve, they do not contribute to making it worse.

Most people *know* life to be a battle and so they gird themselves with all the accoutrement to fight themselves, their fellow man, and everything that *may* happen. They are in a state of constant readiness, always prepared for the worst. They'll beat some one else to a deal, or in a deal. They *know* you can't "trust any one," and "it's every man for himself." Alone, life, for them, is a battle all the way. And yet each one of these individuals feels deeply.

Your point of view

The person who considers life a challenge or a problem draws upon a power to meet this challenge or submit to it. The one who examines life and determines that it holds opportunity regardless of appearances to the contrary relies upon a strength and potential which will produce results in accord with his thinking. Those who reflect that life is uncharitable, a constant encounter engaging them in conflict, combat, contest, skirmish, strife, and an occasional truce, continually draw upon resources that repulse, alienate, compound, and vindicate the stand they take. Each one draws upon—not *"A,"* but *"The* power within" to produce and augment the conditions experienced within and without himself—in his mind, body, affairs, and relationships. By the "power within" he is: alive, animated, active, vital, and productive! Or—he is the seed thought of a fool—the result of his own chicanery. No matter—we cannot live another's life. *But we can live our own.* How and whether and to what extent we do this depends on that shifting quality we call "self-honesty."

We flatter ourselves that we are honest, sincere, and straightforward. And then we delude ourselves for the convenience of the moment. We suggest that we have dreams and hopes to which we would aspire. Then the tall, lofty, elevated, towering allusion becomes an innuendo. There is a test of the honesty of our search and of ourselves: *Do we really want a sense of purpose, dignity, worth and an awareness of meaning? Or are these only words?* Too often our life gives the answer.

Are you willing to make the effort to win?

In a world that is a challenge, in a life that is at times tumultuous and filled with fear, frustration, despair, and unbelievable opportunity to shape, create, and dignify, or distort, subvert, and twist—according to our own design—*are we really willing to make the effort toward a far better expression and experience of mind, body, and affairs?* We are now and always, every moment, faced with substantiating or denying the power within. *How honest will we be with ourselves? How deep is our desire? This is the key that opens the floodgate to the right use of that inner power.* Knowing this is one thing. Specifically, how do we become honest with ourselves and deepen our desire?

What it takes to be honest with yourself

The first test of honesty is: Are you, am I, satisfied with life, our health, conditions, inner awareness of meaning and of spiritual evolvement, and personal relationships? If our answer is truly

"No," then we can stop giving the impression we know more than we do. This will result in an outer quiet and an inner calm, a hesitancy to speak and a readiness to listen. In this moment we are on the threshhold of a whole new life, knowingly attuned to the power within. We are really beginning our search. And in this, there are no words, no questions, no need to ask "What is and where is God; how do I have the things that I would have from life; what is my part; how do I get along with my fellow man?" We are attuned to an inner power and to the realization that *"I am here only to realize and express Christ, and the only possibility of this dawns upon us and desire deepens—not to know answers—not to profound questions—not to be a great mystic or seer—not to change, challenge, or meet life—but to be a living example, a vital experience, and a meaningful expression of life, and in an heretofore unknown way our life says things to us we would not hear before—"IN ALL THY WAYS ACKNOWLEDGE HIM!"* —Proverbs 3:6. *"Whatever your nature you are more than appearance. You cannot know God, or good, or life, or unfoldment—except you would know God and good and life and unfoldment. You know this when you, "In ALL thy ways acknowledge him." This power you seek, this answer you would find—you are this power! You are the answer! "In all thy ways acknowledge him."*

Life does tell us many things. It tells us there is a power and this power is a law within man and all things. In moments of stillness, life tells us this power within is healing, health, accomplishment, failure, success, negation, kindness, gentleness, and misery. *Each and all of these is the power within.* And then, in silence, life no longer tells, but asks, *"What choose ye? War or peace? Love or hate? Greed and destruction? Sharing and abundance? Poetry and kindness? Gentility, creativeness, and good—or bad? The power is within. YOU MAKE THE CHOICE!"*

THE REAL PROBLEM WITHIN US

You and I are a problem. We are pretenders to the throne of reality. We are born and bred to a religion and refuse to abdicate ignorance, for we stubbornly claim that which has been handed down benevolently by the fate that chanced to call us heirs. Our estate is one of wanting that which will acknowledge who we are, and refusing to be receptive to the vast domain of spiritual consciousness.

We look to others and to a thousand things to solve our problems and point the way. Others, in turn, look to us and in a thousand different ways are confused by all that would dispel confusion. The world is much bigger than the projections of the individual. We seek a key to the kingdom, a power of the mind, and a secret to the spirit, and devise ways and means to make dim and dark all that would give light and understanding. We see a pinpoint of light, and like one chasing shadows, we run from one reflection to another. Obsessed to learn truth, we discount the truth of compensation for effort. The teachings we follow are many. The one we pursue to fruition does not exist. Try building a foundation: excavate on this plot of ground, build a wall on that, another in yet a different place—you will never construct a building that way.

Many and varied are the paths to spiritual growth. We may tread upon one and then the other. We must determine a path and follow it to a destination. Or we can do as so very many have done: fraternize with interest, curiosity, and persuasion, but never know that which we seek. We become so enamored by the words of one, or the facade of another, that outward appearance detracts from inner destination. And we walk, and walk, and walk, and never part company with our point of departure.

If you are interested in meaning in *your* life, you can have meaning. You have been and will be presented with many opportunities to know truth. Wherever and whenever you discern that first glimmer of light, *pursue it*. Don't listen, read and talk—*apply*. Make an honest, diligent effort to adopt a principle in your life. Initially there is a benefit in exposure to the worship of others. *Continue to learn a little of this and a little of that, and you know very little of any one procedure.* Set your feet firmly upon a path and *go all the way*— and then you will have the right to say, *"I have sought truth." And with diligent effort, you will know truth.*

YOUR ASSIGNMENT FOR THIS WEEK

"Persevere!" Let this word imprint itself indelibly upon your mind. When you begin to have an understanding that you may find that which you seek, *persevere!* And in that moment of confusion or doubt—*persevere!* When you feel that you have found truth—*persevere!* Now that you have determined to follow a path, let nothing circumscribe, limit, or keep you from that path. *Persevere!*

The secret of knowing God, relating to fellow man, and being spiritually productive is not in being presented with a truth. It is that you have done something with that truth, and in turn that that truth has done something for you.

Now: Each day let spirit guide you to reading a selection of scripture. *Persevere.* Do this each day without fail. Incorporate this scripture into your way of living, thinking and acting.

Concentration and contemplation: Divine consciousness—illumination through spirit—is omnipresent. Wherever you are, whatever the circumstance or condition, apperception is yours if you would perceive—*And persevere.*

In a place of quiet, alone or with another, seated comfortably, back straight, hands in lap with palms upward, inhale as indicated in Lesson (Discipline) 7. Make no effort to clear the mind. Make every effort to concentrate upon one thing: that which calms the mind, body, and affairs. Again, as in Lesson 7, create an image within your mind: visualize a scene that is calm, peaceful and serene. Continue this for thirty minutes daily. That which you are now doing is preparation for all that will follow. You are in preparation for meditation and the Silence. Persevere! Be diligent in that which you do. Persevere—allowing this moment of calm to flow unceasing into your outer affairs and inner activities.

Make note of the changes you observe within yourself and in your affairs.

Conclude each session with a prayer of thanksgiving, being grateful that each experience is an opportunity for spiritual growth.

"Giving thanks always for all things." —Ephesians 5:20

MAKE THIS—

YOUR DAILY AFFIRMATION FOR THE WEEK:

"I am being presented with a truth. I will give that truth an honest examination. For this week and the weeks to follow, my consecration is to that truth with which I am presented."

Your basis for reality
in daily living

At this particular stage of development there is a right path for me to follow. There is little development when I search here and there and scatter my forces, trying first this and then that, and never fully giving any one way an opportunity to prove itself in my life. I must adhere to the principle of being single-minded in my search for God. I know that I can learn through listening, reading, talking, and conversing with my fellow man, but the time comes when I must decide what it is I am going to do, and *direct my life and effort accordingly.*

There is but one power in this universe of spirit. This is not something I use, but something I become so that attunement is a way of life and an expression of my being.

There is but one Being. There are many paths and each man, at different times, prefers one path to others.

"I am being presented with a truth. I will give that truth an honest examination. For this week and the weeks to follow, my consecration is to that which I am presented."

No direct command—and yet—*more than altruistic theory*—We owe ourselves more than the preservation of self. Self-expression growth, and development can only be realized through application motivated by something other than the self. That which is required is of the mind, the body, and the spirit. Our discipline is intellectual, physical, moral, aesthetic, and spiritual—it is realization—and it is up to us. *We can make it more than an idle dream.*

Your self-development questions

Question 1. Relationship is the mirror of discovery. How I relate to the words I read at this moment, the experiences of this or the next moment, and how I act or react, tell me and others much about me. Laid bare for all the world is the kind of person I am and what I am likely to become. *What can you do about each moment of self-discovery in order to not repeat past mistakes?*

Question 2. Each moment of my life I am building, tearing down, contributing constructively or destructively, to everything, every situation, every circumstance, every condition, and every person to which I am exposed. I do this through the power of a mature or immature attitude. If I am mature, I relate—meaningfully. *Imagining that you find yourself in a most unpleasant situation, how would you resolve it and how would you relate?*

Question 3. All of us are sensitive to something. In the poetry of the soul we relate to art, painting, sculpture, sand upon the shore, clouds in the sky, a little child, nature, love, kindness, and understanding. In difficult situations too, we are sensitive. These may lead to heartbreak, frustration, and problems for ourselves and others. The choice is always ours to act or react. Reaction presents the problem and nurtures the power within to expand minor challenges into overwhelming castigation separating mind from meaning and self from others. *There is a path of simplicity which can make the turbulent smooth. What is it, and how would you specifically apply the means and—step upon the path?*

Question 4. Joy, creativity, and expressiveness do not come through effort. When there is a releasing of the self and an encompassing of others, effort fades and a voice, as though not our own, speaks through us—in terms of a giving that receives, and a receiving that shares, and a sharing that must encompass. In this rare moment, poems are written, friends are fashioned, and life is fully lived. *We know these things. Why is there so little remembrance of that which we know will bring that which we and others seek?*

"As in water face answereth to face, so the heart of man to man." —Proverbs 27:19

"STIMULATORS TO ACTION"–

Beyond the word I use is the act I perform—the love that
I am—the truth that I would be.
*   "And the angel that talked with me . . . waked me,*
as a man that is wakened out of his sleep.
And he said unto me, 'What seest thou?'
And I answered . . . saying, 'What are these my lord?'
Then he answered and spake unto me, saying,
"Not by might, nor by power, but by my Spirit."
*   —Zechariah 4: –*
*   Not by the word I use nor by the power of intellect alone,*
but by the spirit an idea is revealed, specific instruction
from within—the act I perform—the love I am—the truth I
*   would be!*

"I bow my knees unto the Father, . . . That he would grant you,
according to the riches of his glory, to be strengthened
*   with might*
by his Spirit in the inner man." —Ephesians 3:14,16

22

How to Profit from Creative Prayer

"CREATIVE PRAYER"

There is little doubt in my mind that man is the only animal that prays–*incorrectly*. I'm also certain there are untold millions who would take issue with the validity or the reasonableness of the statement just made. Let us reflect upon several considerations of this stand of one against many: It would appear a valid premise that man is not only the only animal to pray correctly or incorrectly, but the only animal to pray. It would seem highly improbable that cats, dogs, birds, trees, air or stone represent prayer in any form, or that other animals in nature's vast familial structure could or would pray. Man, being the only evolved creature with knowledge of who he is and his relationship to all life must be the only one capable of knowing God and the power and function of prayer. Immediately we must ask, (1) If man knows so much–is so highly evolved, and prays so deeply, (2) why do his prayers avail him so little? Additional questions must be answered. (3) What is prayer? (4) Is man the only creature capable of praying? and, (5) How does one pray productively and creatively?

What is prayer?

Men's prayers are recognized as many faceted and multiform. We are told that prayer, by dictionary definition, may be "begging, pleading, entreating, supplicating." We are adjured to "Pray without ceasing." (I. Thessalonians 5:17); to "Lift up our hearts and bow down our heads." We are instructed that "solitude and stillness are the way." We "turn wheels and kneel." We "clasp hands and reverently signify the cross by sign." But is this prayer?

Preconceived concepts and long-held ideas tell us little about prayer. Let us consider our questions in the order propounded. We shall reiterate and dispense with each accordingly. (1) If a man knows so much and is so highly evolved, and prays deeply, (2) why do his prayers avail him so little? In the order of presentation: Man does not know so much, is not so highly evolved, nor does he pray deeply, although on occasion his very sincerity contributes to his frustration. If knowledge, sincerity, or what appears an attempt to pray, were all that was requisite, there would be a greater number of happily praying people. We know this is not the case. We can therefore conclude that knowledge and sincerity, though important, are not the answer to prayer. The simplest find prayer an answer. The most educated find the answer only in simplicity. Man, though he does know much about many things, knows neither the meaning of nor how to pray. Accepting the possibility that man may pray wrongly, we can readily understand why prayer avails him little.

In the mind of most men, prayer has its origin in need, desire, want, hope, fear, and frustration. This is neither prayer nor seeking nor receiving what is sought; it is desperation and delusion. *Prayer is not a condition of asking or seeking. It is a state of being—Being in accord!* We presume that we pray when we lack health, money, peace of mind, or order, for it is at these moments of desperation that we turn to that which we call "God." *We are praying when we have health, money, peace of mind, or order—for order is prayer!*

The origin of prayer

Prayer appears to originate in need, while the actuality, continuance, and *creativity* of prayer *is in and through fulfillment.* When you seek, there is no prayer. When all is in order, when there is fulfillment, *this is prayer—and you are praying.* It may seem incredible that you are praying when there is no need for prayer.

It may appear unreal that when your need is greatest—when you strive the hardest—that you are far removed from that which you think you are doing. It must appear equally incredible that man is *not* only NOT the only animal that prays—but *is* the only animal that prays incorrectly. However difficult, we must accept that disharmony is disorder and disorder *is* lack of prayer. *Is there a need to emphasize that order is prayer? And however foreign it may be to our thinking—is it inconceivable that cats and dogs, and birds and trees and stones express, each in their own ways the perfection we seek?*

A dynamic concept of prayer

How does one pray creatively and productively? No one can or must tell you. God intrudes in countless ways, telling us we are in prayer. We look at nature and observe order and harmony. *This is prayer!* We raise our eyes to the blue of sky, and on that rare occasion when there is fresh air, and pure water—each is a prayer. *Prayer is not an attempt to communicate with God nor make things different or better. PRAYER IS WHAT YOU REALLY ARE—WHEN YOU ARE WHAT YOU WERE MEANT TO BE!*

Man *is* creative. In his creativeness he becomes more than the idea. He is the instrument, the idea, the channel, and that which is created. He produces more than the image within his mind. He is productive of subtle, forceful changes in himself, his environment, and his affairs. He postulates a premise: "I can do that which I conceive." In doing this, he becomes what he has conceived.

He may not murmur or lament his lot in life, but he surely must question the effigy of unanswered prayer and seek the manner, means, and method of effective prayer. "The effigy of unanswered prayer"? An effigy is a sculptured likeness or a dummy, that which is unable to respond. In directing our prayers toward that which is wholly intimate, we exclude that which lies beyond.

A creative concept of prayer

Creative prayer is efficacious prayer. Creativity implies causing something to exist which was without shape or visible form. Prior to coming forth in the life or affairs of the individual, that which would be created–*did exist*–in Divine Mind. Prayer, oriented beyond the self, comes forth from Divine Mind *as an effectual concept within your mind and mine.* This is creativity and cannot be separated from creative prayer. We are only creative when we are in communion with that divine "Inner Resource."

There must be few who have not heard of prayer. There are many who do not know how to pray with creative intent. To distinguish between creative and unproductive prayer, we must reiterate that all prayer does produce according to the direction of our life and the purpose of our prayer.

YOUR ASSIGNMENT FOR THIS WEEK

"Thine ears shall hear a word behind thee, saying, this is the way, walk ye in it, when ye turn to the right hand, and when ye turn to the left." –Isaiah 30:21

Prayerfully considering the above scripture, preface your time of prayer and stillness with this affirmation:

"For thy name's sake lead me, and guide me." –Psalm 31:3

And positively listen to these words:

"I will instruct thee and teach thee in the way which thou shalt go."   –Psalm 32:8

And now: *For those who claim that life is governed by chance and fate beyond control, you have the opportunity to prove prayer's creative power.*

At the conclusion of what you might consider your time of prayer, write down ways in which you can make this a continuing prayer, encompassing that time when you ordinarily would believe yourself to be not in prayer.

And in confidence (confidently and quietly) without conscious effort, write down, draw up, inscribe the pattern and the principle (ideas) which will issue forth from this time of silence and prayer–creatively evidencing the manner and means for you to improve your life.

"According to your faith be it unto you." —Matthew 9:29

"If thou canst believe, all things are possible to him that believeth." —Mark 9:23

"Be thou an example of the believers, in word, in conversation, in charity, in spirit, in faith, in purity." —I Timothy 4:12

You can prove your faith. And then,

"Thou shalt see greater things than these." —John 1:50

MAKE THIS—

YOUR DAILY AFFIRMATION FOR THE WEEK:

"As long as there is a need there is a way. As long as one seeks there will be fulfillment. I do seek, and I will find fulfillment."

The basis of reality in daily living

In seeking, I must realize that prayer is productive of whatever I seek. I may pray haphazardly and the results are a jumble of the random, ill-fated, aimless thoughts I have held within my mind without order or purpose. A prime requisite for directive, creative prayer is the discipline of determining positively what I would have, and then channeling spiritually directed effort toward that end. Limitation and frustration are the direct result of misdirected prayer, obscured vision, and failure to determine a correct course of action. A greater happiness and joy is mine when I know:

"As long as there is a need, there is a way. As long as I seek—there will be fulfillment!"

"I do seek and find fulfillment!" For: "The presence of God within me is a limitless reservoir of faith, strength, and power. Each day I express more of His faith and receive more of His blessings." —Silent Unity

Your self-development questions

When we seek to learn the answers to questions we are striving for greater knowledge. We also learn a deeper meaning of relationship in whatever area we perceive the answer.

Question 1. Excluding supplication or form, *give a brief definition of prayer.*

Question 2. *How does one effectively pray for another?*

Question 3. "Theurgy" is necromancy or conversing with the dead. *If religion is not to be a conversation with the dead, how do we make it (religion) a living, vital, present, productive element in our lives?*

Question 4. Discipline, by definition, is "control, diligent practice, punishment, correction, rule of practice." *What does the "discipline of prayer" mean to you?*

"The word of God . . . is a discerner of the thoughts and intents of the heart." —Hebrews 4:12

"STIMULATORS TO ACTION"—

"With thee will I establish my covenant." —Genesis 6:18

Nothing in any talk, book, or teaching will of itself change us—unless and until we are moved to do something with that which we can experience.

WEEKLY PROGRAM
NUMBER
23

The Need to Return
to Principle

Our discourse has been, up to this point, consistent with methods and means of demonstration—of prosperity, health, success, peace of mind, and a spiritual orientation relative to God and fellow man. Several important considerations must be further emphasized.

1. Prayerfully apply the principles presented and your life will change, your consciousness will be elevated, and you will *know,* perhaps for the first time, prosperity, health, and success.
2. God *is* the underlying foundation for every physical, material, psychological, and spiritual reality.
3. All of the books of the Bible contain practical lessons for successful living in every area of life.
4. A partial acceptance of the principles (disciplines) presented will not work. You must accept these truths as though there were no other truth. *There isn't!*
5. You are learning that there is no weak-kneed doctrine called truth. You can know that truth is a powerful, dynamic force with which *you* direct *your* life.
6. These lessons have but one purpose: to help you live an abundant, creative life; to make you a more effective person; to help you become the best person you are able to be on *all* levels of your being: physical, mental and spiritual; *to develop your own innate potential.*

And now . . . let us take Jesus at His word:

"What things soever ye desire, when ye pray, BELIEVE that ye receive them and ye shall have them." —Mark 11:24

YOUR ASSIGNMENT FOR THIS WEEK

Realize: *"Words of wisdom are meaningless to us unless the Truth they are meant to convey becomes a living experience. A truth thus glimpsed, must be experienced and renewed from one day to the next, unendingly, if it is to be fully realized."*
                                                                    —*Ilse Read*
We have come a way upon the path. We were never alone. Now the time has come to join with others—kindred souls.

Daily: Join with at least one other person and read Chapter Five of Matthew (the beginning of the Sermon on the Mount). Read this together. Find the meaning behind each word. Discuss what you have read. (A good companion book is *The Sermon on the Mount* by Emmet Fox)

Now: In the words of the Psalmist, *"Be still and know that I am God." —Psalm 46:10.* Try not to think of conditions either as they are or as you would have them. If you must hold an image, take one solitary object (a flower, a shaft of light, or a color) and concentrate on this.

Remember—a partial acceptance of the principles will not work.

After this week have a friend in attendance with you. During the week, join with this person in practice.

MAKE THIS—

YOUR DAILY AFFIRMATION FOR THE WEEK:

"I stop dreaming of good and start producing good!"

Your basis of reality in daily living

"Today I am going to *prove* my beliefs in the supremacy of spirit and its action in my life as life, health, and prosperity! I am showing to the world my understanding of truth, and I prove it by speaking and doing only that which is positive. I will close this day—this week—knowing that to the best of my ability I have been faithful in proving my trust in the truth to which I have been exposed." *"I stop dreaming of good and start producing good!"*

"By their fruits ye shall know them." —Matthew 7:20

Your self-development questions

Compose *four thought-provoking questions and answer each in the form set out for you in the previous chapters.*

Devise *"A Stimulator to Action"* in the form and shape set out in previous chapters.

WEEKLY PROGRAM
NUMBER
24

How to Demonstrate
Prosperity, Health, Success

One of the first principles of prosperity in any form is sharing. You have arrived at a point where it is essential to have another join with you with whom you can actively work on these principles.

> "Again I say unto you, that if two of you shall agree on earth as touching anything that they shall ask, it shall be done for them of my Father which is in heaven. For where two or three are gathered together in my name, there am I in the midst of them." —Matthew 18:19-20
>
> "If ye abide in me, and my words abide in you, ye shall ask what ye will, and it shall be done unto you." —Jesus —John 15:7

Ask yourself the question: *"What would happen if I completely believed these statements? What would happen if I accepted and practiced ALL the teachings and promises of Jesus? What transformation could I expect in my life and affairs?"* The answer you are able to make to these questions will be the measure of your faith. Your corresponding experience, your mind, body, and affairs will be a manifestation of the measure and application of your faith.

Most men believe in God. So many of us are not certain that we have the ability to contact this source of effective prayer. We can know, despite real and present problems, that God can and will heal and adjust *if we believe and apply faith.* Millions of words are spoken and written about the *"Way of Christ."* They are wasted—unless they lead us personally into a dedicated way of

"discipleship" and *the experiencing of God's presence and promise through our own love, faith, prayer, and commitment!*
"The will of God is divine harmony. We work with it or are frustrated by it. We have the choice: To obey—or pay."

YOUR ASSIGNMENT FOR THIS WEEK

Realize and accept: There is a doctrine of universal principle—more real than objects we sense.

Realize and meditate upon: The nature and fruits of faith.

"Now faith is the substance of things hoped for, the evidence of things not seen. Through faith we understand that the worlds were framed by the word of God, so that things which are seen were not made of things which do appear." —Hebrews 11:1, 3

Daily: Join (this is of utmost importance) with at least one other person and read the Epistle of Paul to the Hebrews, Chapter II, verses one through forty (on the nature of faith).

Discuss what you have read with your "partner in faith" (as covered in a previous chapter program.

In discussing this chapter, use the Socratic method of questioning each other as to the meaning.

Example: "Now faith is the substance ... " Exactly what IS substance? An idea? A concept? A knowing? A certainty? How does one *know* with certainty? You've made a statement—*exactly what do you mean by what you have said?*

"Through faith ... " Through what? Through emotion? Belief? (Belief does not make a thing so!) While belief is an expression of faith, it is not certainty or knowing.

Prayerfully *"Ponder the path of thy feet, and let all thy ways be established." —Proverbs 4:26*

In a place of quiet and comfort, *(with another)* become still. Think not of conditions either as they are or as you would have them. Concentrate on a single object: a flower, a shaft of light, or a color—to the exclusion of all else.

Remember—*This is a discipline* and requires *discipline.*

MAKE THIS—

YOUR DAILY AFFIRMATION FOR THE WEEK:

"I am receptive to new expressions of life. I AM that life!"

Your basis of reality in daily living

"I have faith in the most important time in the world: the present. I express that faith by living NOW. I do not wait for the future—I have the present and I have faith in it! I experience the present by my dynamic, positive attitude toward all things, all persons and all situations. There is absolutely nothing in memory of the past or anticipation of the future that can reduce my faith in nor deny me the privilege of *living this day!*"

"I am receptive to new expressions of life. I AM that life!"

A primary tool—In the wake of that which has gone before, that which follows is meant to exercise the mind. What will you do?

Your self-development questions

Question 1. *Assuming you took the "Affirmation for the Week" to heart and put it into practice, state simply what change or changes resulted in your thinking and in your life.*

Question 2. *Why is God the underlying foundation for every physical, material, psycholgical, and spiritual reality?*

Question 3. *What is God?*

Question 4. *"A partial acceptance of principle will not work." Why is the foregoing true?*

"As thou hast done, it shall be done unto thee: thy reward shall return upon thine own head." —Obadiah 1:15

The Dynamic Power of Thought and Word

No one is poor! We are all rich—*in ideas!* Whether these ideas bring the good we seek or that which we would avoid depends on whether our "rich" ideas obviate, meet and clear away our difficulties and that which is unnecessary, or whether our life and affairs, by implication, proclaim we are rich in an abundance of negativity.

Are YOU rich in positive, dynamic ideas that will produce? If not, determine, now, at this very moment, to be completely and totally positive in *all your attitudes*. It may not be easy, but at least you will have made a start and a step in the right direction.

YOUR ASSIGNMENT FOR THIS WEEK

Of utmost importance: Join with another in your time of prayer, meditation, and serious reading.

Take a positive thought and write it down. Make it part of your day. A good possibility is:

"This is a good day and every thought I have makes it good!"

Now: Each day write down a positive, dynamic thought. Keep these thoughts in a notebook which you carry with you. Soon you will discover that *you are a positive person!* You will have discovered *the creative power of thought and word.*

Realize and meditate upon *the creative power of thought and word.*

A beautiful soul so aptly described the meaning of the creative power of thought and word: *"The word 'utter' and the word 'outer' have the same root meaning. What you 'utter' literally becomes an 'outer' part of your world."* —*Catherine Ponder.*

"Thou shalt decree a thing and it shall be established unto thee . . ." —Job 22:28

"How precious also are thy thoughts unto me, O God! how great is the sum of them!" —Psalm 139:17

Daily: Join (the importance of this cannot be overemphasized) with at least one other person and read 2 Corinthians 10:1-17 and discuss it with your "partner."

Now, in a place of quiet and comfort, (with another) become still. Again, think not of conditions either as they are or as you would have them. Do NOT hold to the image *of a flower, a shaft of light, or a color—but concentrate on but a single aspect of the petal, an element of the shaft of light, or a particle of color.*

"Trust in the Lord (the law of your own being) with all thine heart; and lean not unto thine own understanding. In all thy ways acknowledge him, and he shall direct thy paths." —Proverbs 3:5,6

MAKE THIS—

YOUR DAILY AFFIRMATION FOR THE WEEK:

"I am out-picturing not only what I think of myself, but what I think of God. With every thought I could well ask, " 'Is this what I think of God?' "

The basis of reality in daily living

The greatest truth is neither taught nor learned. The only truth is that truth I live, not tomorrow, but this very moment. And this moment I know that *the present is more than promise—it is fulfillment!*

"I am out-picturing not only what I think of myself, but what I think of God. With every thought I could well ask, " 'Is this what I think of God?' "

Someone once said—"Only a poet has the right and the ability to speak of things of the heart, and of soul, and of beauty." But others have rights as well—and they also have both responsibilities of a thousand shattered dreams and fragments of the life they would have lived. And yet one can emerge from a deeper dream into reality, but a beginning must be made.

Your self-development questions

Question 1. Complete this statement: *"Any who understands divine law is prosperous, with peace of mind and well-being because . . . . "*

Question 2. We are told throughout the Old Testament and the New Testament of the importance of tithing. Whether or not we accept this, whether we know this or not, *tithing is a positive principle of "giving and receiving." If you accept the principle of tithing, state your reasons for knowing this to be a powerful, workable principle. If you do not believe or have never practiced tithing, state your reason.*

Question 3. In seeking to trust divine guidance, *how do we distinguish between it and our own intellect or emotion?*

Question 4. It has been said: "People who are seeking supply should learn the rules of Nature's great Property Custodian and practice both phases of the law of giving and receiving." *What does this mean?*

"As a man thinketh in his heart, so is he." **(AND ALSO ARE ALL HIS AFFAIRS.)**

"STIMULATORS TO ACTION!"–

Interest

Involvement   *All = RESULTS!*

Enthusiasm

" . . . there shall be kindled a burning . . . fire." '—Isaiah 10:16

WEEKLY PROGRAM NUMBER 26

How to Lisen to Build Your Life with Satisfaction

Though we live in a world of sound, noise, and disturbance that is the evidence of building, structuring, contriving, and assembling, these had their beginnings in moments of quiet consideration. Prior to the creation of a sculpture, the object was formed and shaped within the quiet recesses of the mind. Great works of art, paintings, poetry, and the vast world of literature, came forth, not in a crescendo of crashing sound, but in the receptivity of a mind attuned beyond the sight and sound of the world in which we live. In some ways, the world in which we live stimulated the expression that followed. But its real origins were in omnipresent divinity.

By all our straining thoughts and inordinate suppositions, we cannot lay aside the principle of contrivance, and state that cause is corporeal. That which we see, create, and are inspired to meaningfully express, disposes a thinking individual to know that we are not destitute of spirit. One need not be an artful logician or a captious reasoner to realize that God, spirit, periods of silence, and the ability to listen beyond the self produce creative thought, moral action and meaning.

If any of the above is obscure and difficult to comprehend, this is intentional. It is no more unintelligible or disguised than the terminology we use daily, but mostly on Sunday mornings in places of worship. *If we are seeking a better life, health, order, harmony, peace of mind, or prosperity, we are, whether we know it or not, seeking God. And we will find what we are seeking, if and when we know we are seeking God.*

151

YOUR ASSIGNMENT FOR THIS WEEK

For the moment: Release all previous concepts of God, religion, and religious philosophy.

Accept that all of the universe, your life, your mind, your body, and your affairs, though unperceived, are God. All else is concept—right or wrong.

Now: Would you account for the laws of motion, the vibratory essence of sound, the quality of smells and colors, and the course of things? There is a way. And the way becomes a mandate of stillness; an injunction to him who would do more than dream and be more than casual conversation.

In accepting that God is all of your life, your mind, your body, and your affairs—though unperceived—*you have made the first important step toward immediate evidence.*

And now again, become still. Make no effort to think, rationalize, or understand. Give credence to what you are doing. Be still and silent, and accept silently. Listen! Listen and more than the outer ear will cause reflection at a distance to disputations concerning identity and diversity, thoughts and opinion. And a further reflection, originating in and through silent summoning, will allay questioning. You will know the answers. In words of a new awareness, identify what may truly be said of your new awareness.

"Yet shew I unto you a more excellent way." —I Corinthians 12:31
"Having heard the word, keep it, and bring forth fruit with patience." —Luke 8:15

MAKE THIS—

YOUR DAILY AFFIRMATION FOR THE WEEK:

"Beginning this moment, I set aside a few moments each day and become still. In the Silence, I receive inspiration, guidance, direction, strength, purpose, understanding and an inflow of spirit. I am still, quiet, calm, and receptive."

Your basis of reality
in daily living

What is silence? Is it but the absence of sound? No! Silence is the quiescence of all activity. The mind, the body, the world around us—for us, when we are in the Silence—are in repose. We have released ourselves, others, and all things. Yes, silence *is* the absence of sound! But it is also the quintessence of spirit, concentrated essence in purest form of which we can become aware—but only in the Silence.

In the Silence, though we are without thought or action, we taste that which lips have left untouched. It is then that we feel that which cannot be held within the hand, that we see that which cannot be seen with eye alone, that we sense the reality behind and beyond the appearance. It is then that we have listened—and heard.

"Beginning this moment, I set aside a few moments each day and become still. In the Silence I receive inspiration, guidance, direction, strength, purpose, understanding and an inflow of spirit. I am still, quiet, calm, and receptive."

A worthy destination—There is but one reason for success, and that is to have a goal worthy of consideration and to make every consideration worthy of that goal.

Let this be your destination, your goal:

"My thoughts can *build me a dream* of something big. They *now* lead me to a worthy destination!"

Your self-development questions

Question 1. In the world in which we live, there are always countless sights and sounds. If we close our eyes, we create beings, experiences, sight, and these images are all without sound. Without sound, we are divested of the power of "silent sound." Thus we are in a desert of our own creation. *What is your concept of listneing to the "still small voice." How is this done?*

Question 2. It is clear that many will ask, "How can one 'listen' to such an absurdity as a "silent sound"? Yet the thoughts, objects, memories, hopes, and fears within your mind—are they less real than reality? Does not everything start within the mind, even the substance of a solid structure? *Now to balance this seeming imbalance—providing you accept what appears a contradiction—what is it within you that you are listening to? How can you validate your acceptance?*

Question 3. To most of us God is a being omnipotent, omniscient, and omnipresent—yet He seems to have little effect upon us, for God, while remaining incontestable is inconspicuous in the lives of most. Yet God *is* omnipotent, omniscient, and omnipresent, for He is in every sound, sight, thought, and experience. *Silent is the God we loudly proclaim. WHY?*

Question 4. It has been said, "one fails to see the trees for the forest." One also fails to heed that ever-present "sound of silence" in the cacophony of sound. *If you would demonstrate the immense potential within your grasp, your mind, your body, and your affairs, what must you do? And how, specifically?*

"If these should hold their peace, the stones would immediately cry out." —Luke 19:40

"STIMULATORS TO ACTION"—

We all seek answers. Take the concept you do not understand. Observe and ponder it from every perspective. Now give it to God in whatever way you would turn to God. You will find the answer. And you will act!

WEEKLY PROGRAM
NUMBER

27

How to Live for the Greatest Satisfaction

We live by law. In one way or another, penalty is extracted for failure to observe laws. The spirit of the teachings of Jesus Christ is a law of the meaning, purpose, and direction of life itself. We obscure this meaning by looking for something beyond the meaning. *There is no mystery surrounding the teachings of Jesus Christ!* There is only failure to understand what He meant by what He said. For centuries learned men have sought to find the meaning behind the teachings of Jesus. The meaning behind these teachings is stated in the simplicity of His words: *"Wilt THOU be made whole?" —John 5:6. "THY faith hath made THEE whole." —Mark 5:34. "If TWO of you shall agree on earth as touching ANYTHING that they shall ask, IT shall be done for them . . . " —Matthew 18:19 "What things soever YE desire, when YE pray, BELIEVE that ye receive them, and ye shall have them." —Mark 11:24.*

There is a Law. We are compensated by it, we pay the price for breaking it.

YOUR ASSIGNMENT FOR THIS WEEK

For this week, with a sense of dedication, make an attempt to *take Jesus at his word.* Each day read and accept the preceding scripture as complete truth, the truth of your life. Memorize these words: make them part of you. *Your life will express them if*

155

". . . when ye pray, BELIEVE that ye receive them and—ye shall have them."

Now: Accept as the greatest truth you will ever know the words of Malachi, the prophetic critic who placed emphasis on the moral responsibility of the priesthood:

> " . . . Prove me now herewith, saith the Lord of hosts, if I will not open you the windows of heaven, and pour out a blessing, that there shall not be room enough to receive it." —Malachi 3:10

Apprehend and meditate upon the operation of the law in your life.

Consider and meditate upon the effect of acceptance or rejection of the law of your own being. Realize no one can force you to accept or embrace principles that produce health, prosperity, peace of mind, and success. However neither can you escape the consequences if, for any reason, you fail to apply the law of mind *(God—the universal Principle)* action.

Daily, with at least one other person—

Read: The Acrostic Aleph—Psalm 119:1-8. Let the truth of this Psalm direct your understanding:

> "Blessed are they that are perfect in the way,
>   Who walk in the law of Jehovah.
> Blessed are they that keep his testimonies.
>   That seek him with the whole heart.
> • Yea, they do no unrighteousness;
>   They walk in his ways.
>
> Thou hast commanded us thy precepts,
>   That we should observe them diligently.
> Oh that my ways were established to observe thy statutes!
>   Then shall I not be put to shame,
> When I have respect unto all thy commandments.
>   I will give thanks unto thee with uprightness of heart,
> When I learn thy righteous judgments.
>   I will observe thy statues;
> Oh forsake me not utterly."

With your "partner in faith," prayerfully discuss what you have read.

Now in a place of quiet and comfort, become still. Enter the Silence.

This will be helpful in stilling the mind:

" . . . no small sound;
The Spirit hovers near, And—
My mind IS Holy Ground!" —H.K.

MAKE THIS—

YOUR DAILY AFFIRMATION FOR THE WEEK:

"I accept as truth, the law of my being! I put this law into action!"

Your basis of reality
in daily living

The law of *my* being is the expression of God in my life. There *is* a law governing my life. Whether I accept, believe, or doubt—there is a law of being. My acceptance or rejection of this law governs and controls my life and affairs.

The right use or application of the law of my being is the principle of never-ceasing growth and development, producing health of mind and body, abundance and good.

The law of my being rightly applied is the fullness of God: life, love wisdom, substance, and truth in application—*spirit transforming my life and affairs.*

"I accept as truth, the law of my being! I put this law into action!"

Consider this—

"Unexpressed ideas are of no more value than kernels in a nut before it is cracked. We can easily deceive ourselves into thinking that because we possess sound principles and convictions, we are free from any responsibility to pass them on. Rather than let *your* good thoughts "waste their fragrance on the desert air," share them with others, as the Lord has shared them with you . . . it is both your privilege and duty to circulate far and wide the unexpressed ideas *now stored within you.*" —*Unknown*

Your self-development questions

Question 1. *What is meant by the statement, "Know thyself!"? In really knowing yourself, what effect will this have on your life and in the lives of others?*

Question 2. *What is meant by "practical Christianity?"*

Question 3. *How can the intellect build, create, and produce "according to God's plan?"*

Question 4. *What happens when our thinking faculty is "obedient to spirit?"*

> **"Lift up now thine eyes, and look from the place where thou art."** —Genesis 13:14

"STIMULATORS TO ACTION"—

Do you recall—
  What we are interested in, we give our attention to.
  What we give our attention to—we believe in.
  And what we believe in stimulates us to action!
Find a cause
  To believe in.
  Your interest and attention will
  Result in action!

WEEKLY PROGRAM NUMBER

28

The Fruits of Your Expanding Consciousness

An evolving consciousness is a growing, developing, continually changing awareness bringing to bear on life and affairs a directive force producing desired results.

I marshall no argument in defense of the magnificent changes possible when the mind is spiritually oriented and positively directed. To no man can another prove a course of action. Choice is free and the alternative certain. However, because I can construct whatever my mind can conceive, I must ask myself, "Why struggle without benefit—or suffer without consideration?" And then I find that I must determine to *"keep my heart with all diligence; for out of it are the issues of life."* Therefore I choose and accept that faith which gives significance to my life. In place of worry, fear, or negativity, I have hope, courage and determination—and positive results.

MAKE THIS—

YOUR DAILY AFFIRMATION FOR THE WEEK:

"I keep my heart (my mind, soul, and consciousness) with all diligence (constant, persistent attention); for out of it are the issues (all that I experience, know, or manifest) of life." —adapted from Proverbs 4:23
"Keep thy heart with all diligence; for out of it are the issues of life."

Many of us are church-goers

Each one of us has the responsibility of asking. "What can I do to help my church be of service to the community?" Going to church on Sunday must mean more than "listening" to a talk or having a sermon "preached at us." It must mean that each one of us grows in such a way that our church takes on a new meaning in the community, in our affairs, and in the life of everyone with whom we come in contact.

What can you do? If your church is to be meaningful to you, give thought to what you can and must mean to it and to others. Take a friend to church with you next Sunday or to your Temple on Saturday. You will do something for another and for yourself, and your church will grow—in meaning and in the community.

When you go to church, go to the church of your choice. If you don't have a church home, find one—add to it; contribute of your mind, your heart, and your spirit. You will be the better for it.

"Search me, O God, and know my heart." —Psalm 139:23

"STIMULATORS TO ACTION"—

It is time to take religion out of the hush-hush class; . . .every worthwhile enterprise is an act of faith!
    "There is no unbelief; Whoever plants a
    seed beneath the sod and waits to see it push away the clod,
He trusts in God!"
    — Bruce Barton

How the Supreme Law Operates

To truly prepare the soil of the most important aspect of living, I must reflect on several aspects of truth. When I really understand truth, I see God everywhere and in all things. There are two ways of understanding. One begins with faith unfolding the expression of that which he seeks. The other is to combat life with all the forces it seems to array against us.

How to: Demonstrate prosperity, health, and success.

In the preparation of the soil of my life I begin with my thoughts and attitudes. I see God in all things and under all conditions. I "judge not according to appearance," but I "judge righteous judgment." My words, actions, and thoughts are fruit of a cultivated consciousness of spiritual awareness.

YOUR ASSIGNMENT FOR THIS WEEK

In any human or spiritual relationship, prerequisite to and as an antecedent condition, there must exist the element of faith and trust. Relating to other human beings requires our trust before certainty of knowledge. The planting of seed, in the ground or spirit, requires our trust without having seen the results of effort. *Faith is "the substance of things hoped for, the evidence of things not seen." —Hebrews. "Blessed are they that have not seen, and yet have believed." —John 20:29*

In preparation for this coming week, make every thought, statement, and idea, a positive and dynamic expression of *the truth you will prove!*

Now: Determine your own direction by a minus or a plus sign. If your attitude toward anything is positive, it (your attitude) will produce desired results. If your attitude is negative, it will not produce the results desired. Make the plus or the minus sign the determining factor and *know* the soil of your mind will bring forth whatever you plant. You till the soil, you plant the seed, and you reap the harvest. If your mind should question, let this be your question: *"Will this bring forth my good?"*

Recognize and meditate upon: The purpose of your life.

Daily: And of utmost importance—join with at least one other person and . . .

Read: The first chapter of the Epistle to the Hebrews, Verses 1 through 14. With your "partner in faith" prayerfully discuss what you have read and shared.

In a place of quiet and comfort (with another) become still—*enter the Silence. ". . . no small sound; the spirit hovers near, and—my mind is holy ground!"*

"I will plant in the wilderness the cedar." —Isaiah 41:19

"I will set in the desert the fir tree, and the pine, and the box tree together." —Isaiah 41:19

"Plant gardens, and eat the fruit of them." —Jeremiah 29:5

"I have planted, Apollos watered: but God gave the increase."
                                                    —I Corinthians 3:6

"He that planteth and he that watereth are one." —I Corinthians 3:8

MAKE THIS—

YOUR DAILY AFFIRMATION FOR THE WEEK:

"I now identify myself with the rich, abundant life."

The basis of reality
in your daily living

We know that for anything to grow and to come to fruition, there must first be a seed. The only good I can bring forth in my life is through planting the seed of right thinking. An attitude of richness, health, peace, prosperity, and success must be the seed for every thought, every plant, every tree, every dream, every fear, every hope, and every aspiration reproduces after its own kind. It is obvious that we can never plant the seeds of doubt, lack, or sickness, and harvest "the fruit of faith" in that in which we do not have faith.

"I cannot withold and plant fewer and fewer seeds in the hope of a more abundant return. I plant that which is right, good, and meaningful—without fear or restraint—as does nature every moment. Nature receives that which has been given to it and returns to the giver a thousand fold."

"I now identify myself with the rich abundant life!"
"He that tilleth his land shall have plenty." —Proverbs 28:19

Reflect for a moment—

We have and have had all we will ever need. The cave man could have produced what we have today—except that principles were neither known nor applied.

Your self-development questions

Question 1. If you have faith in God, *how can you express this faith to a fuller extent so that you find fuller expression in your life?*

Question 2. *Why must one"feel"a sense of commitment to be a vital part of anything?*

Question 3. Each one of us has the solemn obligation to make the very best and most of himself. *What can you do—right now—that you have heretofore only thought or talked about?*

Question 4. Just about everyone is interested in money, health, peace of mind, and success. *In these lessons you have been presented with "stepping stones" to more money, greater health, peace of mind, and success. Enumerate some of the means presented by which you will achieve what you seek.*

"If therefore thine eye be single, thy whole body shall be full of light."   —Matthew 6:22

"STIMULATORS TO ACTION"—

Envision it! Think about it! Talk about it! Act!
Become what you think!—for you are what you
* have thought.*

WEEKLY PROGRAM
NUMBER
30

How to Sow the
Seed for Success

"Each day of my life is a cultivation of thought, a sowing of the seeds of whatever thoughts I accept, and I must accept the fruit of these thoughts, for I have planted these seeds in the soil of my mind. No other individual, no circumstance or condition does this for me. The blame, the credit, and the choice are entirely mine. What I do with this day should give me nothing but great joy, for I know it is mine to do with as I will. Therefore I sow the seed of happiness; I build dreams into reality; I live a life of vibrant health and abundant prosperity. I cultivate these thoughts! I sow the seed! And I reap the reward—for "I do believe ALL things are possible to him that believeth."

"I am an example of the believers, in word, in conversation, in spirit, in faith." —I Timothy 4:12

How to: Demonstrate prosperity, health, and success.

The sowing of seed is analogous to the law of tithing. In order for the individual planting a field to receive, he must be willing to give. Both in tithing and planting there must be a willing, open, and receptive mind. In planting and in tithing, the giving of the seed or the tithe (time, money, or ideas) must be completely in faith. The farmer and the tither both give and at the moment of giving have no visible signs of return. In tithing and in planting the principle is the same: that which is given or shared must be a just and fair proportion of that which has been received. In tithing, one gives ten percent. In planting, we can well imagine what would occur if the farmer planted fewer and smaller potatoes.

165

"I recognize the abundance of life! I expect and accept only the good! I receive the good! And I share the good I have received!"

YOUR ASSIGNMENT FOR THIS WEEK

Enthusiasm! The very word itself has a ring about it denoting action. In a thesaurus we discover that "enthusiasm" is the expression of great feeling—"feeling, willingness, hope, love." Wherever there is a feeling toward anything there is an acceptance, a warmth, and an earnestness. Willingness, in its truest sense, means but one thing; proper acquiescence which again means but one thing—enthusiasm, zeal, and readiness! Hope implies desire and promise, and most certainly aspiration. Love? Attachment, devotion, and passion!

This coming week make whatever you say, do, and think an expression filled with enthusiasm. Be enthusastic! Speak with feeling! Accept with love, warmth, and hope! Express *now* a new kind of passion and excitement about everything and everyone.

Now: Be prepared for new and exciting reactions from those around you as you sow the seeds of an enthusiastic attitude.

Give thought to the seeds you sow each day. You will realize why your experiences have been "fruitful" according to the "seed."

Daily, join with at least one other person and—

Read: Chapter 30 of the book of Isaiah, Verses 18 through 26. With your "partner in faith" prayerfully discuss what you have read. (The importance of joining with another cannot be overstressed.)

In a place of quiet and comfort (with another) become still—enter the Silence. Seek to expand your consciousness to an awareness of the Christ within all. Seek to be transformed in spirit, soul, and body by the "renewing of the mind."

"And he will give the rain for thy seed, wherewith thou shalt sow the ground, and it shall be plenteous." —Isaiah 30:23

MAKE THIS—

YOUR DAILY AFFIRMATION FOR THE WEEK:

"I am receptive to growth and an expanding expression of the limitless expression I am!"

The basis of reality
in your daily living

"I have a choice! I make this choice! I make the explicit, positive choice of bringing forth more good in my life than I have presently. I *know this seed* thought will *produce* when I am receptive to growth and the limitless expression I am!"

"The seed that will come to fruition is the seed I plant from the choice I make. I now, this moment, make a clear choice to live by faith, absolute faith in God. When I base my life in God I live with faith, I know hope, and I express positive ideas!"

"I am receptive to growth and an expanding expression of the limitless expression I am!"

"And I, if I be lifted up from the earth, shall draw all men unto me." —John 12:32

The true function of words

It has been stated that we use words as vehicles to bring us closer to that which is within the mind, or stimulated from outside ourselves. But words are only vehicles. An automobile carries us on our journey toward a given destination. Words, as vehicles, carry us toward God, our fellow man, and understanding. But both words and any other conveyance are only something that take us toward our destination. It is important that we do not lose sight of our destination in our manner of approach.

Your self-development questions

Question 1. A number of qualities or characteristics are necessary to success in any endeavor. *List them and then state why you believe your list to be accurate.*

Question 2. The clergyman's responsibility is complete and total dedication and consecration to the ministry of God, and service to his fellow man through man's relationship to his fellow man and his desire to make life meaningful with that which he feels within his heart and from "something" he feels both within and without.

Enumerate ways in which your role as a responsible being parallels that of the minister, priest, or rabbi.

Question 3. The right to truth, to evolving and understanding, is every man's right. Touching upon truth, he takes upon himself a responsibility. *What is this responsibility?*

Question 4. Albert C. Knudson, Dean Emeritus of Boston University School of Theology, stated in *The Principles of Christian Ethics,* (page 189) "Without freedom . . . there could be no adequate self-directed effort toward the attainment of the divinely appointed goal of one's life." *While this is true, what limitation does freedom place upon every truly free man?*

> **"Let us not therefore judge one another any more: but judge this rather, that no man put a stumbling block or an occasion to fall in his brother's way." —Romans 14:13**

"STIMULATORS TO ACTION"–

"By acting today, your dreams will not recede into
the mists of tomorrow.
So take your thought, your dream, your hope, your aspiration
of yesterday and today and plant it deep
in the soil of the ever-present now—
this very moment!
By acting this very moment, you walk in
the company of the great—for it is the truly great who act!

How to Gather Your New Abundance

In the Lord's Prayer we say, *"Give us this day our daily bread." —Matthew 6:11.* This is a truly beautiful thought. It is much more than an expressed desire. It is a law of reciprocity. It is a law of mutual exchange, cooperation and maturation. We, as the seed planted, receive as we give. We do not obtain merely for the asking. Our "harvest" is as bountiful in growth as are we generous when we give. We live and receive in direct proportion to the unselfishness of our love for others and our desire to give to them *their* "daily bread." In the ratio of self-interest, personal gain, and concern for none but ourselves, our harvest is apportioned. Let us *pray,* not *say, "Give us our daily bread."* In this way prayer becomes a practical reality, a planted seed, and a harvestable crop.

How to demonstrate prosperity, health, success. Religion, a way of life, and an understanding do little unless they are productive of the fruit giving meaning to that which we have given of ourselves. Religion, matured, became a way of life through the man we call Jesus. He nurtured the soil, trimmed the vine, and brought forth the fruits we fail to harvest.

The central theme of all that Jesus gave can be comprehended by its own simplicity: *Choose ye this day whom ye will serve." "Each produces according to its own kind." "As ye sow, so shall ye reap."*

I would that you would affirm with me with certainty, *"God gives me all I am capable of receiving. My mind, my desire, and my commitment to the acceptance of the living truth alone determines the wealth of the harvest—or the poverty of my*

169

thinking. My mind, my body, and my affairs, with God, are well-springs of total abundance."

YOUR ASSIGNMENT FOR THIS WEEK

We talk *of* spiritual values, illumination, growth, maturity, and understanding. What we are seeking is the fruit of the endeavor, an advantageous result for our effort. The degree to which we maintain our sense of the eternal and its implications in your life and mine depend entirely upon our maturity. In this we are like the crop: there is a time of planting and a time of harvest. This is the growth to maturity.

Up to this very moment we are harvesting seeds we have planted. This we shall continue to do as long as we live. Only from this moment on *we will choose, select, and plant only that which will bring forth an abundant harvest from mature ideas.* In the minutes, moments, days, weeks, and months ahead, reach forth and grasp higher expectations of yourself, others, and all things.

Now: Admit that a person has to be mature to be responsible as does a crop have to be mature to be of value. Recognize that every moment and every situation presents opportunities for immature or mature actions, attitudes, and judgments.

Realize, meditate upon, and produce a plan to make your maturing process a plan for growth of the mind and expression of the spirit, with breadth, depth, and continuity conducive to *health, peace of mind, prosperity, and whatever else you would have.*

Daily: and with at least one other person, read the Epistle of Paul to the Colossians, Chapter One, Verses 1 through 19.

With your "partner in faith" prayerfully discuss what you have read, inquiring into its depth.

In a place of quiet and comfort become still—enter the Silence. *"Ponder the path of thy feet, and let all thy ways be established." —Proverbs 4:26*

"The harvest truly is plenteous, but the labourers are few."
—Matthew 9:37

MAKE THIS—
YOUR DAILY AFFIRMATION FOR THE WEEK:
"I accept myself as the fruit of God's abundance!"

Your basis of reality
in daily living

For every fruit there is a season. There is a time for planting, a time of cultivation, and the time of harvest. To "harvest" is to gather that which has been sown, the product or the fruit of one's labor. Knowing this, "I produce the fruit of God's abundance *only* when I sow the seed of that which I would harvest."

"My actions, my words, my thoughts are the fruit of prior actions, words, and thoughts. My affairs are the harvest. This awareness is evidence of my choice of the seed sown and the harvest gathered"

"I determine that my actions, words, and thoughts shall become "visible fruit" of God's abundance and evidence of my spiritual understanding causing the image in God-Mind to become 'visible' in my life and affairs."

"I accept myself as the fruit of God's rich abundance!"

"As the branch cannot bear fruit of itself, except it abide in the vine; no more can ye, except ye abide in me." —John 15:4

There is a way—

There is a way to live so that you will be successful in every area of your life. What you do with that which is and has been given throughout your life is a "Step Upon the Path." You are learning some of the rules of life and its living. *Will you apply that which you are learning?*

Your self-development questions

Question 1. Paul, in I Corinthians, Chapter 12, Verses four through forty, enumerated many of our spiritual gifts. We may conclude that "healing," though not the greatest gift is truly a "branch of the vine." —John 15:4. *If a person has had healing power and it seemingly leaves him, why should he not regard this change as a loss?*

Question 2. What does the following statement mean to you? *"The grace of God is an inheritance that tells us we shall share the beauty, love, and kindness of all men and shall bear not the measure or mark of any except ourselves."*

Question 3. We cannot *wish* ourselves into oneness with God. *As we have to physically transport ourselves from one place to another, there is a definite procedure to follow in order to "enter the Silence." What steps are essential to "practicing" or "entering" the Silence?*

Question 4. Many never hear the "Voice of God" because they expect only an audible sound, as of another human voice. God "speaks" to us in various ways; as intuition, as a knowing wherein there is no doubt, as an idea, or as an inspiration. We must learn to listen. *If a close personal friend competely rejected the above, what would you say and do (providing you accept this)?*

"There are, it may be, so many kinds of voices in the world, and none of them is without signification." —I Corinthians 14:10

"STIMULATORS TO ACTION"–

Maturity means "completion in natural growth."
Intellectually, maturity means intelligent action
in any given situation. Spiritually,
maturity is the dignity of God—the divinity of man!
"If you know these things, blessed are you
if you do (express) them." —John 13:17

WEEKLY PROGRAM

NUMBER

32

How to Build Your
Storehouse for Success

"Concerning thy testimonies, I have known of old that thou hast founded them for ever." —Psalm 119:152

"In the wide arena of the world, failure and success (peace of mind, health, and prosperity) are not accidents as we so frequently suppose, but the strictest justice. If you do your fair day's work, you are certain to get your fair day's wage—in praise or pudding, whichever happens to suit your taste."

—Alexander Smith, Dreamthorp,
"On the Importance of a Man to Himself"

In ways without number may we interpret that to which we have been exposed. And though we may interpret a thousand things in a hundred thousand ways, there are but two procedures we follow in application: we either comprehend or fail to understand; we benefit, or we lose; we apply truth, or we live less than we are. In no manner whatsoever do we change, alter, or avoid the consequences of our understanding.

Each of has a vast storehouse of knowledge, ability, experience, and opportunity from which to draw. Draw forth the wonderful resources of mind and spirit! A stored harvest is of no value unless and until it is taken out of storage and put to use. *"A man's life consisteth not in the abundance of the things which he possesseth."* —Luke 12:15, *but of the abundance he has to which he puts to use.*

"Concerning thy testimonies . . . thou has founded them forever."

173

How to: Demonstrate prosperity, health, and success.

There are many things in life to which we are entitled. We are heir to all we can embrace—all we have drawn to us in a consistantly sustained acceptance. We are that which we have drawn forth from the "stock-shop" of a destiny we have determined. Those who claim life, health, peace of mind, and all the rest to be governed by chance are expressing little more than pagan philosophy—a ritual of nonbelief.

YOUR ASSIGNMENT FOR THIS WEEK

Deal with your destiny with a positive, practical application of the truths with which you have been presented.

Meditate upon and substantiate the following: Great moments of inspiration exist in the life of every living, thinking, aspiring human being. On rare occasions, seemingly without effort, a poet is inspired as spontaneously as a bird in song. All too seldom, a masterpiece may come forth—again, seemingly without labor. *Everything,* even these moments of inspiration, comes forth only because one has striven, worked, and sought for an elusive word, the perfect phrase, the expressive sound, the right color, the correct meaning—a hundred thousand times before.

Whatever you would have—this moment, right now—begin. Start by thinking of health, peace and rich abundance. You may not be healthy today nor have the peace of mind you seek, but consistent, sustained, spiritually directed thought will produce very real health, peace of mind, and abundance in your life—and the way to achieve them.

Daily: And with at least one other person—*PRAY!* Know that when you ask for a cup of coffee you are not served tea. In every area of your life you also get what you ask for. If you will settle for less, you will receive exactly what *you* will draw forth.

Read: Chapter 12: Verses eleven through twenty-three of the Gospel according to Luke.

With your "partner in faith" prayerfully discuss what you have read.

In a place of quiet and comfort (with another) become still—enter the Silence.

"I would seek unto God, and unto God would I commit my cause." —Job 5:8

MAKE THIS—

YOUR DAILY AFFIRMATION FOR THE WEEK:

"I have a vast storehouse of knowledge, ability, and opportunity! From this moment on I shall draw forth the wonderful resources of my mind!"

Your basis of reality in today's living

From the moment of our birth and through each continuing moment of life, life provides each and every man with countless experiences, manifold opportunities, and a continuing chance for self-realization, growth and development. There is always not only the storehouse of that which we have learned, but the total accumulation of knowledge, inspiration, wisdom, insight, understanding, direction, and guidance of the inspiration of those elevated to a measure of accomplishment. And we can well know this: "Whatever others have accomplished, I also can, if I but will—achieve. I have the creative power of a mind, spiritually directed and oriented to express inner potential."

"I have a vast storehouse of knowledge, ability, and opportunity! From this moment on I draw forth the illimitable resources of my mind!"

"Thou preparest a table before me . . . " —Psalm 23:5

Do you not know— Unless the idea you have, the book you read, the challenge you meet results in your taking up the idea, the book, the challenge, and doing with it that which is constructive, there is little difference than if there were no idea, no book, and no challenge.

Your self-development questions

Question 1. It has been said that "God never gives anyone more than he can bear." *If this statement is valid, why do we have so* *many examples to the contrary; i.e., those with serious drinking problems, suicide, uncontrollable action (violence), etc.*

Question 2. What is the first prerequisite to an "awakening" so that one can have peace of mind, health, and prosperity—*and know a new sense of oneness with all creation?*

Question 3. In effect, when we have tithed and it has not "worked" for us, we are saying: *If God does not "honor" my faith, then I no longer will give him what I am told is his share until I make certain of my share." What is wrong with this statement and our approach?*

Question 4. What did Jesus mean when He said, *"Blessed are the poor in spirit"?*

> **"The law made nothing perfect, but the bringing in of a better hope did; by the which we draw nigh unto God."** —Hebrews 7:19

"STIMULATORS TO ACTION"—

"Be ye doers of the word, and not hearers only." —James 1:22
"Faith, if it hath not works, is dead." —I John 3:18

**The vision beyond
of things to come**

It has been said, "There is nothing more precious than time." There is one thing equally as precious as time: *what we do with time.* Some few, all too rare individuals, do wondrous things with the time they have.

Give thought to the wondrous works of art, literature, beauty, and meaning in the world, because some few have done the most with what they have—the very same time you and I have. Perhaps they were able to live a creative life, filling it to abundance for us because they gave so little thought to themselves and so much thought to what each man has the choice of doing. They looked with eyes and heart and mind with a sense of love that they must express in words, painting, producing, relating, a love and a zest for life itself and for the most inconsequential of things and the 'most important of all things—*each individual moment, seeing in it a rare opportunity to take from life the best it has to give—and in return, giving back to life the very best they have to give.* I truly believe all of us like to do this very same thing: to contribute to life, to draw from life, to know that each day has a fullness it might not have had, had we not done that which we did do.

What is it that makes the profound difference in him who would "do" and "have" and "be" and in him who *does* and *has* and *is?* A number of things and yet only one. Not whether we paint or write or create, because we all paint, even those who never held palette or brush in hand. Upon the canvas of life we are always adding shadow, tint, and hue. In the Book of Life, we constantly enscribe our hopes, our fears, our failures, our frustrations—and our willingness to accept life as a wonderful challenge—or as a devastating, heart-rending, destructive experience. Thus we create our own world, marvellously wrought—or something less. But what is it that makes the most profound difference in him who would "do" and "have" and "be," and him who *does* and *has* and *is?* It is something we have heard about all our lives, something we have touched upon. It is something we have "turned to." *That which makes the most profound difference in our lives, what we are, what we would be is: how much time we spend in prayer.* This has little to do with the prayers we say, or the church we attend on Sunday, or whether we read the Bible in the evening. People talk about the formality of prayer. What I am talking about is *a life of prayer* where every act, every deed, and every consequence is of *consequence,* where everything we think and do is God-oriented and spiritually directed.

How do you live a life of prayer? Remember Brother Lawrence and what he said? *"I lived life as though there were none but He and I in this world."* Remember the passage from the Book of Proverbs, the third Chapter and the sixth verse? *In all thy ways acknowledge Him."* This is prayer in its purest form, removing doctrine and dogma, and leading us to a vision far beyond where most men stand.

The true way of life

Too often we seek pat answers to growth, evolvement, a better life, and a solution to our problems and reject that which is different from the patterned program of previous acceptance. We know prayer as a formality. I say, *know prayer as a way of life and you will know positive living through creative prayer*. The average thinking, seeking individual does not want theology as it has been given. And yet we find him asking us not to change anything—but to change everything. "Give me words, manner and means of changing my life." I talk to you in words, leaving out ecclesiastical terminology. Do you feel there is no religion? We speak of prayer and limit prayer to the formality of a doctrine and a dogma rather than a direction. Yes, words move us, but a living experience moves us more. Walk upon the desert floor in the early morning. This is a living, vibrant experience. Stand upon the deck of a ship alone at night watching stars upon the sea, and the sea and sky and ship becoming one—this is a moment in eternity. It moves you. I don't think anyone wants neat little dogmas. I do believe most thinking individuals want practical food for thought and stimulators to action. So that this discipline is more than merely listening or reading the thought of another man, I ask you to embrace a discipline. All of us know what we are saying to God. Will you undertake a task? With paper, pen, or pencil write down, *"What is God saying to me? And in what ways?"* Then, *"God's purpose for me is"* And *"My responsibility to all with whom I come in contact is . . . "* The last task set before you at this moment is to turn to Psalm 37, verses I through II. Read prayerfully and then write an interpretation in your own words of the deeper meaning you find. You will have made good use of your time. You will have understanding of prayer. And you will have begun to live *through "The Vision Beyond."*

WEEKLY PROGRAM
NUMBER
33

How to Know the Simple Path to Your Success in Life

Life is immensely complex but beautifully simple. Its implications are enormous. Frustration, fear, superlative growth, insight, understanding, desire, fruition, desperation and despair are but part of the complexity. Quiet, meditative moments are more than moments of self-realization and self-revelation. Possessed of and by the infinite, the self recedes and that which was unimportant becomes recognition of all that is important. One has set his foot upon the path of reducing complexity to meaning, comprehending the incomprehensible, discovering beauty in what was heretofore thought ugly, crass and chosen to be avoided, ignored, and dispensed with.

Purpose cannot come through intellectual urgency or pursuit. By every act and thought we traverse a new distance upon the path to purpose—a step closer or a margin wider—bringing us to or separating us from our goal.

Too long, the concept of the individual has been denigrated with referral of accomplishment to generalities: mankind, or the masses. You have within you all you will ever need to accomplish, perform, create, and express. *But you must know this.*

We talk of love and are lonely. We vocalize our need to be one with our fellow man and separate ourselves from him by the very words we use. We accent our desire to the elegance and purity of spiritual awareness and contemn, confute, diffuse, and fail to discern the elegance and purity around us. We voice the need to create and do not realize that all we know is the creation of our own confusion or comprehension. We are the spokesman of the gods of our own creation and the voice of the God who gave us mind and choice. We expect others to do for us that which we must do for ourselves—love, relate, and seek. We choose, create, and walk upon the path. *What path choose ye?*

YOUR ASSIGNMENT FOR THIS WEEK

To understand the power, potential, and possibilities which lie within requires exercising the power of your own mind. Quote Christ, scripture, Buddha, Sri Ramakrishna, the life and teachings of others, and you have barely touched the meaning possible for you to know. These men and minds are guideposts, examples, and expressions. The answer lies in personal experience and expression, not in quotations and reference to what others have said or done.

The discipline to use: It is important now to not allow the body to intrude upon the mind. In concentration, this is the first difficulty to overcome. Assume a comfortable position, keep your back straight, hands resting in lap, palms upward, and breath as indicated in Discipline 8. The purpose of body position and manner of breathing is not a magic path to spiritual understanding or inner awareness: it is necessary, though, to the elimination of distracting influences and reduction of strain in concentration and meditation.

Stilling the mind and body, relax, release, and again, in a receptive mood, accept within your mind the peace and tranquility of the wave upon the water, a bird upon the branch of tree, or a cloud in the sky gently passing by. Dwell upon but one of these representations of peace and tranquility. Let time drift by. Maintain this mood for a period of twenty minutes. With each succeeding continuance of the discipline of concentration and realization, there will be renewal, a constancy of concentration, a lessening of thought of time and effort, a deeper awareness and a gratefulness for the path unfolding before you.

Record the changes in your notebook you observe in mind, body, and affairs—and the changes you are beginning to anticipate.

MAKE THIS—

YOUR DAILY AFFIRMATION FOR THE WEEK:

"This day, each step I take will be a path of purpose. By design and intent I make genuine my resolve to contribute to life."

Your basis of reality
in daily living

It is a paradox that as we tread upon a path, we fashion the very path upon which we walk. We may wait for the right path, the precise moment, a particular opportunity. We wait in vain—for the pattern, the standard, or the contingent time is always now, at this moment, in this place, in this circumstance.

In seeking to change conditions of mind, body, and affairs, we change nothing by seeking to change conditions of mind, body or affairs. In our determination to find life, in a moment of quiet introspection, we find we have run from life. In our effort to get something from life, some few learn that to get, one must give. In our attempt to lift the veil that abscures, we deepen the darkness.

How, then, shall we find that which we seek? We must change, not circumstances, conditions, or others, but ourselves. We know the meaningful things of life: kindness, sharing, understanding, love, compassion, gentleness, and interest. Know that others seek and faint and falter as do you. A first step on the path to purpose—giving purpose to the path—is to give the very thing you seek. If you would have ideas, give your marvelous mind an opportunity to construct, develop, and share *your ideas* with others. If you would dispel loneliness, share the love you would receive. Determine: *"This day, each step I take will be a path of purpose. By design and intent I make genuine my resolve to contribute to life."*

The hidden meanings
in your life

The depths of life, their hidden meaning, and the inspiration which they bring are revealed when we place our faith and trust in something other than ourselves. It is then we can take hold of life in a true and forceful way; it is then we do not doubt. Instead of looking for the meaning of life, we know we are, ourselves, that meaning.

Your self-development questions

Question 1. An English author, Christmas Humphreys, observed: "The habit of meditation is a necessity for all who have taken their own development in hand. The need is recognized in the more spiritual East; it is far more necessary in the material West. . . . " *How can one transform the "need" into action?*

Question 2. In every religion is much that is profound. However, any religion is but one school of thought. Direction is given, precept presented, doctrine shared, and emotion stirred. If this is all that is accomplished, religion becomes an escape from the unpleasant realities of life. *You know that life, religion, and associations are made up of "give and take." From what you have been given in your religious philosophy, what are you going to return to life, religion, and your fellow man?*

Question 3. In things of the spirit, most teachers, masters, and gurus welcome those who will sit at their feet in adulation. In an effort to be "saved" by "he who knows," all too often the earnest, interested, seeking disciple becomes enslaved to another's egotism. *As one who seeks the path to purpose, how shall you find that path?*

Question 4. The purpose of these questions is twofold: 1.) To make you think, and, 2.) To assist you in unfolding within from a growing awareness of all that is without and within. *State and share (with another) your thoughts which will be helpful to others seeking light upon the path.*

"In all thy ways acknowledge him, and he shall direct thy paths."
—Proverbs 3:6

The true path to purpose

The path to purpose, to God, to meaning, is sharp, clear and well defined. It is not made up of words, quotations and aphorisms. It is not made up of buildings, organizations, and groups, nor is it made up of a church without people relating. The path to purpose, to God, and to meaning is made up of individuals relating on a person-to-person basis. The path to purpose? Each moment of our life we come to a crossroad. You and I know all that is necessary to have purpose to our path. But we must walk upon that path.

"STIMULATORS TO ACTION"—

Incorporate these words into your daily thought:
"Am I doing my best?"
    With every experience ask,
    "Is this my very best?"
Wherever you are, silently query:
"What more have I to contribute, share, do, or be?"
Not only will you dignify your relationships—
    you will act according to
    An honest answer.

"Provide things honest in the sight of all men."
                                  —Romans 12:17

WEEKLY PROGRAM
NUMBER
34

How to Select the Building Blocks for Your New Life

Thought is a creative force. However thought alone will not produce a desirable condition—unless our mind relates to a condition that is desirable. When we think of a "creative" force, we are apt to accept that anything "creative" is good and productive only of good. In this we err. *Thought alone will not produce a desirable (worthy) condition—unless our mind relates to a condition that is desirable.*

Consider the words of Charles Fillmore concerning the creative force in man, from the book *The Revealing Word: "Spirit-mind is the creative force constantly working in man and all other creation. Those who fail to recognize Spirit-mind shining within them dwell in a continuous state of darkness and ignorance. To them the almighty Christ (each person's potential perfection) is nonexistent." "And the light shineth in the darkness; and the darkness apprehended it not." —John 1:5*

A further examination of creative force indicates the importance of selective thought: Creative—"bringing into being; cause to exist; give rise to." Force—"the capacity by any means—mental, physical, psychological, to bring about change; hasten growth of." The recognition that you and I continually utilize creative force to build or block, for good or not so good, should be most apparent. That the choice is entirely ours is set forth in scripture:

"I have set before you life and death, blessing and cursing; therefore choose life, that both thou and thy seed may live." —Deuteronomy 30:19

"Seek ye first the kingdom of God, and his righteousness; and all these things shall be added unto you." —Matthew 6:33

"Blessing I will bless thee, and multiplying I will multiply thee." —Hebrews 6:14

And— *"Except the Lord build the house, they labour in vain that build it. . . . "* —Psalms 127:1

The greater life, the greater God, the building stone, must be a wider vision and a deeper view, encompassing broad horizons and endless possibilities for oneself, God, and the world in which we live.

YOUR ASSIGNMENT FOR THIS WEEK

Commit to memory the scripture quoted in this lesson. And then, *know* the depth of the meaning of that which follows:

There are three aspects of the creative force of mind and spirit. One is positive; one is negative. The third is our choice.

On the Plus side:	*Choice*	*On the Negative side:*
+		
God	⟵——————⟶	greediness
vision		blinded view
hope		fear
involvement		withdrawal
accomplishment		frustration

The list could go on indefinitely. For every evil there is a counterpart. We do the choosing. The building materials? Spirit, mind, and everything with which we come in contact.

"How long halt ye between two opinions?" —I Kings 18:21

MAKE THIS—

YOUR DAILY AFFIRMATION FOR THE WEEK:

"May I, every moment of my life; feel every moment to be a time of truth, responsibility, and duty—truth to be found in every situation; responsibility so that I know the meaning of truth; and the recognition that full use of whatever talent I have, I possess for a greater purpose than self alone. This is truth recognized, responsibility accepted, and duty fulfilled."

Your basis of reality in daily living

Few indeed would doubt that mind is a creative force. The first essential of insight is productive use of this force. Used creatively, the mind is a self-consistent, directive influence. The accomplishment of a people or the evolving consciousness of an individual is the result of passion and enthusiasm—truth recognized, responsibility accepted, duty fulfilled—collectively or individually—for a greater purpose than self alone.

In every philosophy are the building blocks of life or that which blocks the building of a life. As in chemistry, similar elements blend, unite, and become one. Thus it is with that to which our mind relates. Thought colors the act. What we fear, believe, hope, and aspire to—is charismatic of your life and mine—each building a block, or—a block to building.

"Every moment of my life is a time of truth, a period of responsibility and performance—full use of the talents I possess—for a greater purpose than self alone."

The art of practical believing

If you believe in a thing and it is worth living for, it will live for you. Pursue it. If you do not believe in it—forget it.

Questions for self-development

Question 1. *"I would seek unto God, and unto God would I commit my cause; . . . "* —Job 5:8. In the seeking, questing heart of Job we have a positive approach to life and its living. In the words of William Wordsworth we have the rancour of man's failure to find the "Truth."

"Look for the stars, you'll say that there are none;
Look up a second time, and, one by one,
You mark them twinkling out with silvery light,
And wonder how they could elude the sight!"

In seeking to know the truth, cite factors persuasive to action which would stimulate one to: *1.) Read the Bible, 2.) Better himself, 3.) Be involved in church or other activity, and 4.) Do rather than dream.*

Question 2. If upon awakening tomorrow morning you were to learn that the right to attend church, discuss religion publicly or privately, or read the Bible had been taken from you, *what power and presence in your life would come to the fore—and in what manner?*

Question 3. For the success of any endeavor there must be a clear-cut plan of operation and action, and a goal. Included are incentives that will promote participation on the part of those within the structure. *Write down that which will embody a greater area of service by you and by others in any organization of which you are a part.*

Question 4. The environment best suited to bringing a human being to increased awareness and a richer life is not one that remains uniform, comfortable, *and static,* but one that gently stimulates reception and adjustment to change. *Involvement, for most people, would be both dramatic and histrionic. How would you involve people in that which interests you, your church, its growth, its services, and its needs?*

"There is neither Jew nor Greek, there is neither bond nor free, there is neither male nor female: for ye are all one...." —Galatians 3:28

"STIMULATORS TO ACTION"–

Whatever stands between desire and fulfillment is dissolved by the intensity of desire—sustaining the image—and fulfillment.
"If therefore thine eye be single, ... " —Matthew 6:22

WEEKLY PROGRAM
NUMBER
35

How to Structure the Foundation of Your Great New Life

While it is possible to build machines that can learn in a very real sense, man, the builder, all too often experiences the frustration of being able to teach while lacking the ability to learn.

One thing to note. To build, construct, and create, man must have communion beyond the self—must be "in tune with the infinite" (Trine) in some manner. It may seem difficult to realize that souls are "made," and characters are "formed" upon the choices made each moment, each day. These choices are made by the individual concerned. The responsiveness of the individual, appreciation, a sense of urgency, and an awareness of commitment are unique within each individual as there is variation in handwriting, fingerprints, color of hair, eyes, skin, and other physical characteristics. Each and every human being differs not only in some ways, but in many ways. However, whatever we would build, construct, or create, must be built, constructed, created upon one foundation—that which lies beyond the self.

Upon the veil of a mask: Most individuals have asked the question, "What is the purpose of my being here on this earth?" This question can only arise out of deep need and lack of fulfillment. Resultant inadequacy corresponds to the veil or mask we construct as the result of a foundation that will not sustain, hold up the image, the dream, or the desire we say we have. Upon what shall we build? Scripture points the way:

"The righteous is an everlasting foundation." —Proverbs 10:25.
"Righteous" implies right relations.

Say what we will, do what we will, there is a right and a wrong way of doing everything. A bridge built according to sound engineering principles (with right relations of sand, soil, use, and material) will serve the function for which it was constructed.

A life, your life and mine, are more than a tragic fact. Beyond the veil there is that within, beyond and, above man, more than that which seems to turn his finest qualities into something less than good and his sincere endeavors into failure. *Call it what you will, this is God!! A relation to God, bearing kinship with man.*

YOUR ASSIGNMENT FOR THIS WEEK

Through conscious effort each individual can come to realize that the complexities of life need not be overwhelming. Proper thought patterns will produce the proper result. *Make this your second affirmation for this week: "Proper thought patterns will (and do) produce the proper result!"* Think on this and choose wisely what you will project into your affairs. You are, by your patterns of thought, producing events in your life, conditions in your affairs, and expressing health, happiness, abundance—or their opposites.

For this week: Examine the qualities you most admire in another. Emulate, strive to equal or surpass these qualities as you incorporate them; make them part of that which you are, rather than that which you admire in another.

Spiritual Values: Daily, read and meditate upon the third chapter of the Book of Proverbs (in its entirety).

"There was silence, and I heard a voice." —Job 4:16

MAKE THIS—

YOUR DAILY AFFIRMATION FOR THE WEEK:

"My life, like clay, is something I can model, shape, and form. My environment and all that I experience are the materials with which I must work. Faith is both the foundation and the substance. Knowing this, I shape and form my life according to the design of my own choosing."

Your basis of reality
in daily living

At times we may wonder at the pattern of our lives. We may question the lack of meaning, paucity of results, or effort without sufficient reward. It is right that we question, for there is no need to accept life "as it is." There is no need to accept life for less than we would have it, for with a pattern and the proper foundation—conscious awareness of that which lies beneath (in the subconscious mind)—we raze that which we have built which has produced results not to our liking.

"There is One Life, receiving what we give, restoring what we need. We are a part of this Divine Development."—Evelyn B. Bull, The One Life and its Living

"My life, like clay, is something I can model, shape and form! My environment and all that I experience are the materials with which I must work. Faith is both the foundation and the substance. Knowing this, I build my life upon the firm foundation of faith deep in God and elevated in me—elevating me to new heights."

Wisdom—

"Rendered to the righteous a reward of their labour, guided them in a marvellous way, and was unto them a cover by day, and a light of stars in the night season."—The Wisdom of Solomon, Chapter 10, Verse 11 (The Apocrypha)

Your self-
development questions

Question 1. To accomplish means to "bring to pass; do; complete; achieve." "Accomplishment" means "performance; attainment." (a) *As a result of the series of disciplines up to this moment—what have you brought to pass, done, achieved, performed, or attained?* (b) *If the results have been negligible, what do you believe the reason to be?* (b) *If results have been forthcoming, state your reason for these results.*

Question 2. Our capacity to evolve is inherent but our ability to *evolve spiritually* depends on that which we discern spiritually. *What is the difference between "spiritual capacity" and "spiritual ability?"*

Question 3. Every human being desires something better for himself. Betterment cannot be lasting nor satisfying except that it involves you and contributes to the betterment of other human beings. *What are your suggestions concerning the manner in which you can effectively contribute to this betterment? What commitment are you able, willing, and ready to make?*

Question 4. There is a basic attrition, a wearing away, of much within the framework of every church and religion that can give meaning where meaning is sought. This is not due to lack of human or spiritual resources, but a denial of our responsibility of oneness—a refusal by individuals to apply significant effort. When people, individually or collectively, "withdraw" by lack of participation and involvement in any action or movement from which they "receive," they deny essential human relatedness and deprive themselves of the very good they seek for themselves. *After prayerful consideration, ask yourself, "Am I part of the problem or part of the answer?" "Do I really give that I may receive?"*

"Behold, I am with thee according to thy heart." —I Samuel 14:7

"STIMULATORS TO ACTION"—

Understanding of words—and meaning to life—
   "Purport": profess; seem to mean.
   "Purpose": intend; intention; aim.
"Purposeful": determined; resolved; serving a purpose.
   "Purposely": deliberately; intentionally.

"Ye shall seek me, and find me,
   when ye shall search for me with all your heart."
                                        —Jeremiah 29:13
"Except the Lord build the house,
   they labor in vain that build it." —Psalm 127:1

How to Have the Vision
Beyond Human Eyes

What are you? A quick and ready answer—Man? Woman? Native to or of a certain country?

You are a distance! You are as far as you can see! What are you? *You are a sounding!* You are the depths of how, when, and what you feel! What are you? *Most certainly not a blasphemy.* For you are right or wrong—but only in understanding. What are you? Are you the dreamer? Or the dream?

What are you? *You are all men—differing only in degree.* For you are me and I am thee, and we are the distance of the vision separating or uniting. What are you? You are God—in every aspect, in every part—*but not in whole.* What you are of God depends upon how far extends your vision, how deep you feel, and how and where and when.

What are you? How well you know exactly what and who you are! But memory fades in moments of despair, and we seem other than we are when burdened with a care. But we know what and why we are, for there are moments of greatness in even the least of us. In these moments, far and wide and deep, we see and feel and care—for in these moments how well we know that God is there.

What are you? There is no need to ask. There is a need, reflective, of the Omnipresent, and in this reflection there is contemplation in which each sees the self-same image rather than distortion caused by time of day, difference due to where the observer stands, or previous experience coloring that which is looked upon.

It is not ignorance that beclouds our vision, for this is far beyond the physical. Transcending the observation of the mind, the vision "beyond" is a function of the spirit. And to all men, *spirit* remains the same, regardless of mind's acceptance. Most certainly in gazing upon a lake we may one moment see it blue, or green, or varied shades and hues. A moment later, from the vantage where the observation first was made, it may yet another color be. *But the lake itself remains the same.*

YOUR ASSIGNMENT FOR THIS WEEK

Our view of life must now be joined with life itself. In this there is no variable, shifting, inconstant perspective. Our observation, of necessity, is of spirit and spiritual discernment. Isolate the concept, the idea, the person, the place, or the thing? Each embraces and influences the other; each influences you, and you are an influence. Thus simple thought accepted begins the balance of *the Vision Beyond.*

Allow yourself to perceive, regard, and examine the running stream of consciousness that is the rhythm of nature which does not divide, but is the universal process.

In this relationship, with little thought, you will perceive that which inspires the highest ideals—that which is the essence of poetry, art, music, and which is the cause of sight and sound. Acutely you discern the world in which you live.

What you are seeking now is beyond the power of the intellect alone. The infinite cannot be narrated in finite terms. Something within will tell what words are unable to say.

Continue your search in silent acceptance that you are one with all that is. Devote twenty to thirty minutes daily to this acceptance.

Record how deeply you feel that which may not have been felt before.

"Let me go over, and see the good land that is beyond. . . ." — Deuteronomy 3:25

MAKE THIS—

YOUR DAILY AFFIRMATION FOR THE WEEK:

"I am not a puppet in the hands of fate. I have the ability to see beyond whatever appears to be. With this vision, I step forward in faith—to a destiny of my own making."

Your basis of reality
in daily living

How cruel we are to ourselves. We hear a sound, we see a sight—and we embrace them for what we think them to be. We determine what they are: If they appear frightening and looming large, then so they are. We stand in defense of we know not what, by giving signification, and do not see that which needs emphasis. One of the most inspiring experiences of consciousness is to penetrate beyond that which seems to be, beyond the force and power of thought, to that which is the source of thoughts, things, and appearances.

We are provided with all we ever need. But we must extend our vision to realization. There is joy, harmony, beauty, and self-determination in the realm of spiritual discernment. It becomes us to touch upon that which cannot be seen with eye alone.

"I am not a puppet in the hands of fate. I have the ability to see beyond whatever appears to be. With this vision, I step forward in faith—to a destiny of my own making."

Your self-development questions

Question 1. George Berkeley, Bishop of Cloyne, in his *Treatise Concerning the Principles of Human Knowledge,* published in 1710, refers to an earlier work, *Essay Towards a New Theory of Vision.* In this, he states: *". . .proper objects of sight neither exist without the mind, nor are the images of external things, . . . in strict truth the ideas of sight, when we apprehend by them distance and things placed at a distance, do not suggest or mark out things actually existing at a distance, but only admonish us what ideas of touch will be imprinted in our minds at such and such distances of time, and in consequence of such or such actions."* He further elucidates, *". . . that visible ideas are the language whereby the governing Spirit, on whom we depend, informs us what tangible ideas he is about to imprint upon us, in case we excite this or that motion . . . "* Bishop Berkeley is saying,

"Whatever comes into being is from the source of Spirit, *and that something is required of us.*" *What is it that is required of us to extend the "Vision Beyond" wherever we might be in consciousness or physically?*

Question 2. We cannot direct the action of that which we call God. All we can do is orient ourselves so that *that* which we call God *directs* our life. *How can this be done with greater effect?*

Question 3. When the mist of appearance is swept away we see things in a far different perspective. While dreams and visions that we hold appear far from reality, *why is it important that we both hold to a far vision and let not appearance (that which we could term "reality") shape the vision?*

Question 4. (a) Among many of the mystics, an attitude of mind is "thinking only of God." How does one "think only of God?" (b) This question is one that requires much thought and consideration. We know that man's perspective of God varies with understanding, acceptance, and religious exposure. *Knowing this and knowing that those "thinking only of God" would "think" in different terms, how does man think in terms of God that is consistent with "thinking of God?"*

"He that cometh to God must believe that he is, and that he is the rewarder of them that diligently seek him." —Hebrews 11:6

"Some have entertained angels unawares." —Hebrews 13:2

"As for me, I will behold thy face in righteousness." —Psalm 17:15

"STIMULATORS TO ACTION"–

You would be moved? What touches you? Reach out—
And touch it then!
Action! Power! Life!
All these are vibrant, moving,

Makings of the one who would but live.
You would be moved? What touches you?
Reach out and touch it then.

WEEKLY PROGRAM NUMBER

37

How to Have Fulfillment of Your Dreams for a Great New Life

In preparing for life, a speech, a trip, or improvement of the mind and affairs, the first and basic consideration is the objective. Whether or not we succeed in what we are contemplating can be determined in terms direct and proportionate to the method we use, and our determination to attain the goal we have set. The measurement of results is implicit in the effort expended.

Because so many people have difficulty formulating a plan of action, adhering to "the dream unto fulfillment," it is important to consider means to achievement. The rules are few: the admonition: keep them short, clear, and in your mind.

1. Objective, goal, desire? As in a public delivery, the speaker must ask himself (and know the answer), "What am I saying?" You must ask yourself, "What do I want?"—and know the answer.

2. Achievement? Again, the speaker must question and determine "how best will I communicate that which I have decided to discuss?" You must question, determine, and seek out how best you will accomplish and attain that which you have set before you as a goal.

3. Eat, drink, sleep, dream, and *live* that which you are seeking. Make what you want important enough to do something about—other than merely talk.

We don't need many rules to achieve. But we do need determination, enthusiasm, and a burning desire to do that which we all too often give lip-service to, and do nothing about. It is obvious that "talk is not cheap." For if we talk and fail to do, we fail to find fulfillment of our every dream.

The means to effective living contains but one limitation: That which we place upon ourself by an attitude of mind, or the failure to determine a goal which, in turn, circumscribes desired results. The means to effective living, suitably stated, to the point and purpose, are in the inclination of a mind attuned to God: *"The keys of the kindgom are in the hands of the man or the woman who is aware that Heaven is not a place but a state of mind." – Lilian Lauferty, God Keeps an Open House p. 228.*

One wonders why a man will pursue a shadow and ignore the substance he has within his grasp. In most areas of life we find examples of individuals reaching out, seeking, and striving to find meaning, riches, and happiness, while all the time, within the grasp of each individual, is the substance (mind and spirit) which will bring him meaning, riches, happiness, and health—and yet the shadows are pursued.

YOUR ASSIGNMENT FOR THIS WEEK

Read: Chapters Thirty-two and Thirty-three of the Book of Job.

After reading: A time of prayer, silence, and serious consideration of *how* these words may apply constructively in your own life.

Write them down. Your understanding will be the principle of a clarified goal.

A thought to ponder! With insight to stir the depths of our unrevealed souls, a beloved friend of Kahlil Gibran tells us "we are yet babes in the arms of our children."

> "The mother sleeps at night with the lump of flesh she calls her son sleeping at her side—that lump of which she knows no more than does a water-tap about the water flowing through it: What it is, whence it comes and whither it goes, and what the purpose is of its coming and going. Were it permitted her to touch the hidden threads of the spirit that tie her babe to thousands of men, women and children then walking the earth, and to thousands yet unborn—and this writer among them—the wonder and the shock would surely overcome her."
> —Kahlil Gibran, A Biography, by Mikhail Naimy

> "They make you that ye shall neither be barren nor unfruitful . . . ."
> 2 Peter 1:8

MAKE THIS—

YOUR DAILY AFFIRMATION FOR THE WEEK:

"I face this day and its challenges, and accept the opportunity to be more than I may have been. I will genuinely pay a compliment, extend a tribute, and share an honest feeling of good I have toward another. Failing to have this feeling, I will look beyond appearance, knowing that as I do, I will produce a good effect, emulate the man called Jesus, and though I may do no great good for some—I will be that exceptional one in a thousand. My good shall return unto me.

Your basis of reality
in today's living

Possibly the deepest fulfillment of an individual's dream is to know that he is wanted, needed, appreciated, and loved.

As he may have a responsibility to me, I most definitely have a responsibility to him. In all the little things that might be left unsaid—if I genuinely feel them, I will no longer just feel and think them. I will express them in the many ways always before me. These unsaid values are as necessary to others (as they are to me) as the air breathed, the food eaten, and the renewal so important through rest.

The importance of these thoughts expressed extend beyond the expression into inspiration, appreciation, kindness returned, understanding, gentleness—and the fulfillment of a very deep need of every human being to be wanted, needed, appreciated, and loved. And this is exactly what you will receive for what you have shared.

Most of us love, need, want, and appreciate others to some degree or extent. Most of us fail to share these thoughts and feelings. If I would face this day and its challenges, and accept the opportunity to be more than I may have been, I must ask myself, "As I hope to be wanted, needed, appreciated, and loved—have others reason to expect less from me?"

"One man among a thousand have I found . . . ." —Ecclesiastes 7:28.

Your self-development questions

Question 1. In the field of medicine, all too often in recent years we have come to hear an all too familiar word—"malpractice." How much of the accusation is justified or is acuity on the part of an individual to make an easy dollar is not for me to judge. "Malpractice" is defined as "improper conduct, especially by a physician." In intellectualizing reasons why we have not that which we have every right to have, we have made concessions in conduct—we are culpable of "malpractice." We have persuaded ourselves that "spirit" is of secondary importance. *In what specific manner can you reduce the all too human mistake of "improper conduct" in regard to the importance of spirit in your life, and recognition of this self-same "spirit" in all others and in all else?*

Question 2. To the one who peruses these lessons with comprehension, it is obvious that one without an idea related to God which inclines to action rather than theory is one who has a talent and does not use it. *Most spiritually oriented individuals know that spiritual orientation extends far beyond the words we hear, read, or use. If you have attempted to put truth to work in your life and the results have been negligible, what do you believe the reason for failure to be?*

Question 3. A second referral to Charles Fillmore and his book, *The Reavealing Word:* "Intellectual understanding of Truth is a tremendous step in advance of sense consciousness . . . Spiritual understanding is the quickening of the Spirit within. Spiritual understanding is the ability of the mind to apprehend and realize the laws of thought and the relation of ideas one to another." *We know what is required of us to intelligently understand things of the senses. How do we understand spiritually?*

Question 4. No one can deny the importance of the intellect. With our mind we create, fashion, form, change, shape and devise the world in which we live. Without the mind we would vegetate and be no more than the plant in soil. Yet, with our mind, we also create much that would better be left to that void absent of thought. *What must be done to discover within ourselves that flow of thought which evolves independently of the reasoning process* *and is the constant whisper of the soul saying, "Hearken to what I have to say and all the world is yours!"*

"Even in the frustration of my hopes I see the hands of God." — Quotation from Islam

"Say not, when I have time I shall study, for you may perhaps never have any leisure."—Judaic teaching

"STIMULATORS TO ACTION"—

"Start moving!"
"How many ideas, aspirations, intents and dreams have you had that never materialized?
"Know why? Very simple:
You were distracted by a tempting, seductive, little hussy named Procrastination."

"Ask your friend Noah Webster about her. He will say, 'Oh yes. She almost kept me from finishing my dictionary. For 36 years I battled her from the time I started until I finished. I interpret her as meaning: "to put off from day to day." She comes from a large family. I know her sisters named Defer, Delay, Retard, Postpone, and Prolong. She also has three little brothers named Tarry, Dawdle and Dally. And friend, if she gets into the front seat of that car with you, you will never get out of the driveway.' "
—Bob Conklin, The Dynamics of Successful Attitudes, p. 167.

**A reflection on the tie that
releases you from what you are
to what you would be**

There can be little doubt in the mind of a more than casual observer that a speaker or a writer attempts to persuade his listening or reading audience to an agreement with him—to solicit a change of perspective, and the importance of this changed perspective to the individual.

The reasons for this solicitation will vary with the speaker or writer. Behind whatever the approach, the message is very nearly uniform—the change you accept will be to your benefit. All promise something for you. The speaker or writer's motives determine the value of that which is expounded. The first assumption is that you, as part of a particular audience, have a need. The second assumption is that you are somewhat desirous of change in some area of your personal persuasion, or that you can be petitioned to a cause. The third assumption is that you can be induced, morally, psychologically, monetarily, or intellectually, to accept that which is presented. Politically invested interests stake careers and vast sums of money on the premise that you will be persuaded by a promise.

Poets, artists, painters, and other creative individuals rarely have such a motive. They do that which they must do—and in some subtle, unseen way, changes are wrought in others. The speaker or writer has to be completely unmasked as to intention *if our purpose is to be served.* In like manner, we have also to strip ourselves of casual intent and purpose, and accept purpose with intent. Divesting what we hear and read of all except the bare essentials—individually—we have to determine what is right or wrong, with or without value. And then we must decide what to do about it.

You and I know, of course, that the history of mankind is replete with individuals seeking something. So speakers and writers have a ready-made market *if the product they are selling is sex, politics, money, prestige, or a thousand other things that inflate the ego.* "All that is sold is yours for the asking. Easy and without effort. All you have to do is buy the book, back the persuader, or subscribe to the doctrine." Unfortunately it doesn't work that way. Sex, for most people, is something they read or fantasize about, or see in the movies. Too often politics is promises and little else. The money you are going to make and the prestige you are going to achieve *you have to make and achieve via your own efforts.*

Religion has less to fall back upon and demands more of the individual. People want questions answered. More often than not, the very nature of the questions return the questioner to the very center of the problem—and the very center of himself. We can try in countless ways to find peace of mind, solace in time of loneliness, understanding, a light in the depth of darkness, *but we must return to the self.*

How to meet your challenges
head-on

Your problems and mine, your challenges and the challenges which confront me, the opportunities for betterment we both seek, are not abstract and elusive; they are simple and direct, and they involve changing concepts and systems of values. The concepts we must change involve acceptance and application of informed perspectives of the past. *We must listen to and abide by the words of a man called Christ.* The system of values most important to alter concerns your worth as an individual, and a transformation to that value. Consider what this means. First, if we are not honest with others—and most of us aren't—we must be honest with ourselves. We recognize that there is much more we can do to develop our minds to depart from that which produces unsatisfactory answers direction in life. But even more, if we are to dignify that which we say we are "created in the image of," we have to reach a point in our lives and thinking where we make the momentous decision to do something about ourselves. We have to determine that today—this moment—NOW!—is when and where I begin!

We know the consequences of theory. Would we know the truth of harmonizing spirit—to be found right where we are? If we would—what can we do?

We can form a new theology based upon an old religion— *primitive Christianity.* This "new" theology radically differs with the fundamental belief of modern Christianity and orthodox Judaism that man, and man alone, is created in the image and likeness of God *and is a special creation of God.* This is man's idealization of himself to the degradation of all other forms of life. Perhaps his greatest hindrance in knowing his own value and meaning is in not recognizing the value and meaning of all other forms of life. An attempt can be made: beginning today, look beyond the surface—at others—at things—and hold in greater esteem even the air you breathe.

It was posited earlier that religion has less to fall back upon than persuasion. Religion's greatest persuasion is not in religious books, pamphlets, or talks upon the subject. It lies within the heart of the man who can say, "Nothing less than the best will suffice for men;" the one who knows the significance of going from a reflective to an objective. The evidence, relevant and positive, is not in lectures, books, words, dreams, plans, hopes, or schemes—*but in him who wants. The greatest salesman is he who seeks—for he has found!*

How to Know the
Responsibility You Have
for Yourself

Immanuel Kant advanced the observation that "Man as a person belongs to 'the kingdom of ends' precisely because the end he himself pursues and the means whereby he pursues it are not set for him but are freely appointed and freely chosen by himself!" This places upon the individual the responsibility of facing himself for what he is and what he experiences, and the favors of fortune—good or bad.

The proposition that you and I have and exercise "freedom of choice" presents us with more than rudimentary reasons for responsibility of this choice. There are ethical principles involved in the pursuit of whatever our goal—for our goals always comprise intricate relationship with our fellow human beings. The dignity of the individual too often involves the indignity of other individuals because his "freedom of choice" is a demand limiting freedom of choice for some few or many.

The only choice you have

To the extent you and I recognize involvement in others' concerns, we lessen problems, countenance facts, and know ourselves in the light of what we are and what we can be; but we must remove the mask of freedom of choice. There is no choice—only the determination to do that which is morally right, ethically correct, and spiritually channeled.

How we do this depends not on the religion to which we

adhere, the church with which we affiliate, or the God we claim as our own. The way in which we proceed, progress, and comprehend, evolves through effort to raise our consciousness above the apparent and elevate others to a place beyond appearance, separating man from man and self from God. This last awareness is the source of all other rights and the only concept making any man right, good, kind, loving, relating, or spiritual. To the extent we know this, we reduce knavery, discriminate, comprehend, evolve—and receive that which we seek. We are completely unmasked, and we are the better for it.

YOUR ASSIGNMENT FOR THIS WEEK

To produce, one must have knowledge of that which is desired, and then apply principles to produce consequences. Let us begin by considering that which is sought, and then contemplate whether the value extends to others or applies to the self alone. Should your deliberation inform you it is for you and you alone, not even you will find it to your advantage.

Now: After determination, know that no area of your intention need lie wasted, uncultivated, or unproductive. Face yourself for that which has hindered and for the tremendous possibilities which lie within you. Without reservation, accept the power and potential you and others have to evolve. Admit you have complete and total responsibility for your own evolvement, and in this evolvement always the opportunity to sustain another along the way.

Relax. Breathe in deeply—hold the breath. Exhale. Repeat for a few minutes this drill of preparation.

In quiet contemplation envision yourself upon an island with a gentle breeze: a place of peace and quiescent tranquility. Embrace the moment as a reality and a living experience. Let your mind, body, and affairs drift off as upon the clement air. Relax; release; let go.

Slowly, without effort, allow that which you have decided to concentrate upon take over. Hold to this image, not by effort of will, but by the gentle persuasion of a relaxed mind, a body at peace, and affairs that are in order.

Maintain this as a daily reminder

"With loving kindness have I drawn thee." —Jeremiah 31:3

MAKE THIS—

YOUR DAILY AFFIRMATION FOR THE WEEK:

"I set before myself perhaps the most difficult of tasks. I look for Christ where the human seems to be. I seek to express the Christ (that which is God-like) from within myself. With others, before I speak, act, or judge by appearance, I become still and listen to a sound beyond the sight. I look for Christ where the human seems to be."

Your basis of reality in today's living

We live in a world of practicality. Bills must be paid; clothing is a necessity; we must travel by car, by foot, or by other means. The world in which we live requires that we eat, sleep, and rest.

In this world, we differ widely from one another. There are Catholics, Protestants, Jews, and many other forms of spiritual individuality, and there are individuals within these categories. The subtle forms masking the fullness of each one are infinite and not always visible. Know this: "The task I set before myself, though difficult and formidable, is possible and profitable."

"I look for Christ where the human seems to be. I seek to express the Christ from within myself. In others, before I speak, act, or judge by appearance, I become still and listen to a sound beyond the sight. I look for the Christ where the human seems to be." Beyond all this there is the presence of God!

Your self-development questions

Question 1. Among the several definitions of the word "simplicity," we find "freedom from complexity or difficulty." Few people know us as we really are, for we conceal our deepest self behind a veil. The result is the complexity we appear to be and the difficulty we know in relationships. *Being truthful, most reveals us for what we are. This sometimes causes deep hurt to another. How can we ever and always be truthful and yet not be unkind?*

Question 2. We live in a world of trees, birds, wind, sky, and sea, and countless other things. The greater the complexity, the less awareness we have of the world in which we live—and our relationship to it. *Knowledge and academic background have little to do with appreciation or apperception—one must be sensitive. Complexity breeds insensitivity. How can you keep from living superficially and without sensitivity to the world around you?*

Question 3. As important as it is to be honest with others, it is of equal importance to be honest with ourselves. As a result of self-honesty, self-awareness will compensate for the "devastation" of truth. *What can and will you do to face the reality of inner truth and self-realization?*

Question 4. We have inferred that to really remove the mask of complexity hiding reality from fiction and self from discernment, one must be honest and express sensitivity through simplicity. *A mind dedicated to pursuing truth, meaning, and purpose is far from simple. How would you resolve the apparent inconsistency in the above?*

"Let a man examine himself, and so let him eat of that bread, and drink of that cup." —I Corinthians 11:28

"STIMULATORS TO ACTION"—

*Play a role. In your mind change places
with someone with whom you wouldn't change places.
Make a genuine effort to understand how you would feel if
you were he or she.*

*With understanding will come a far different attitude.
Your action will be
An attitude of the heart—
Compassionate understanding.*

WEEKLY PROGRAM
NUMBER
39

How to Let Your
Consciousness Evolve from
Where You Are Standing

"Theology is sometimes accused of giving elaborate answers to questions which nobody in fact wants to ask."
                              —F.B. Barry, What Has Christianity to Say?

We might add: "Intelligent people will often ask questions for which there appear to be no answers." And, perhaps, less articulate individuals, with yearning heart and soul will exclaim, *"Why me? Why has this happened to me?"*

Consider this: There are no questions without answers. There are no problems without solutions. There is no seeking without *"The Way."* How often we ask questions believing there is no answer!

An evolving consciousness is an unfolding awareness, a *knowing* beyond the emotion, experience, and question—an answer to the seeking. If we wish order, there must be an orderliness to our thinking. If we seek richness in our life, there must first be a richness in consciousness. A question, whether articulately phrased or less expressively formed, should be honestly answered. All who seek are entitled to answers. There is only one purpose for this series of lessons: to give meaning where meaning is genuinely sought; to help you find answers sought.

Several considerations are of consequence: Can beauty, love, understanding, knowledge, wisdom, or accomplishment be expressed or brought forth through indifference? Neither can we have insight nor an evolving consciousness without consistent

208

patterns related to a definite goal or object. The books of John, James, and Proverbs reiterate the foregoing consideration:

"Faith, if it hath not works, is dead." —I John 3:18

"Be ye doers of the word, and not hearers only." —James 1:22

"The soul of the sluggard desireth, and hath nothing; Hope deferred maketh the heart sick; But when the desire cometh, it is a tree of life."

"Every prudent man worketh with knowledge; . . ." —Proverbs 13:—

One's aspirations are vain indeed, if one believes that the good things of life—health, direction, peace of mind, prosperity, spiritual understanding, and success—will come forth simply because they are wanted. Insight, productiveness, fulfillment, and reward all grow and develop—they cannot be given simply for the asking. Inspiration, God, and poetic influence may beckon to a man—but the man himself must reach out, take hold of, and do something with what has been proffered.

YOUR ASSIGNMENT FOR THIS WEEK

Foundation for an evolving consciousness: Meditation—spend some time each day in continuous and contemplative thought.

Begin the discipline of daily practice of "a time of quiet." Promise: *"I will establish my covenant with thee." - Genesis 6:18*

For this week: In every way possible put into actual practice the meaning of the words in Verse 22 of Psalm 22.

"All that is within me, bless his holy name." —Psalm 103:1

MAKE THIS—

YOUR DAILY AFFIRMATION FOR THE WEEK:

"My first responsibility to others can only be expressed in and through the awareness I have of my responsibility to be, do, and express all I am capable of doing and being. In this I look to no other man. I am the example! God is the inspiration! I am the expression!"

**Your basis of reality
in daily living**

There is temptation to view reality totally from one's own perspective—"from where one stands" in relation to "time, space, and events." To fulfill our responsibility to ourselves and express capability, we must "know" reality, walk upon "the path," and be the "light" by a conscious effort toward that end and nothing else.

Reality is a state of actual existence—truth!

"Realization" is cultivation of eternal values, an expanding consciousness producing that which is sought.

"The Path" extends beyond the vision, allowing the truth of spirit to dispel the fog of wrong perception. The "Path" is the power or law to which we must be attuned. This we must view, not from where we stand, but by the light of divine experience.

**Know this for your unfailing
support:**

"My first responsibility to others can only be expressed in and through the awareness I have of my responsibility to be, do, and express all I am capable of doing and being. In this I look to no other man. I am the example! God is the inspiration! I am the expression!"

Your self-development questions

Question 1. We speak of "consciousness" as being aware of various aspects of life. *Enumerate at least twelve different "states" of consciousness.*

Question 2. Many books have been written and courses taught on how to be successful, how to achieve health, healing, and peace of mind, and how to be a success in life. None of these appear to be a panacea, for we always have individuals buying the books, taking the courses, and continuing in the same slough of ill health, want and disturbance. *What do you consider the one basic fault, not of the book or the course, but of the individual?*

Question 3. "To the measure that man is free, God is limited both in power and in foreknowledge." *A deep meaning lies behind this quotation. What does this mean to you?*

Question 4. One man "sings the song of the soul," another "paints the artistry of the gods," and yet another "speaks a language beyond the sound of words." *Precluding so-called inherent differences, what reason would you give for the great disparity in talent, ability, and success, and the rewards of one and the oppression of another?*

"Whatsoever ye do, do all to the glory of God." —I Corinthians 10:31

"STIMULATORS TO ACTION"—

Principles—to be effective—
must be applied.
   And

     "As the marsh-hen secretly builds on the watery sod, Behold I will build me a nest on the greatness of God: I will fly to the greatness of God as the marsh-hen flies in the freedom that fills all the space—twixt the marsh and the skies:"

     By so many roots as the marsh-grass sends in the sod—I will heartily lay me ahold on the greatness of God."
             —Sidney Lanier, "The Marshes of Glynn"

     "Shall thy wonders be known in the dark? and thy righteousness in the land of forgetfulness?"—Psalm 88:12

The real pattern of an evolving consciousness

Now I will give you part of the real pattern of the plan of an evolving consciousness so that you can, if you wish, enrich your life this very day. That which is suggested is so simple that you may not recognize its importance in your life. You may not want to do it, but that will be your loss:

Take a pencil, pad, pen, or whatever is at hand. Go into any room of your home, or outside. Examine a familiar object. Near me at this moment is a song book. It is approximately five and one-half by eight

or nine inches in size. The cover is green with flecks of gold which
reflect the light. My reaction? The green begets a multiplicity of past,
present, and possible images. I think of the green of nature and its
life-giving chlorophyl, of the grass, the bird, the tree, and that "we" are
"each other, I and thee." It brings to mind that circulating medium—
money. And money brings to mind flecks of gold, golden sunsets, and
the times and places I have been privileged to see the sun set—and those
with whom I viewed this splendor. Within the covers of this book are
the creative expressions of the minds of men and women of other times
and places. Their thoughts, the notes, lines and words—emotion moving
spirit—come forth from them—to me.

Is the picture clear?

Now select a familiar object. Examine the shape, size, and
dimensions. Initially it is important to consider the familiar, for it
is the familiar we take for granted. Pick up a leaf, a bud, or a blade
of grass. Write down, not *the,* but *your* description of it—the
angle, shape, form, contour, color, and feel of it. Look upon a
friend, a vase, or paint on the wall. What substance colors or gives
character to this friend or familiar entity? What is it that makes
this what it is? Take a cup—the cup from which you drink your
morning coffee. Hold it in your hand. Really examine it. Turn it
upside down. Visualize the substance from which it was made, the
earth and area from which it may have come, the hand that first
designed it, the personality behind the vessel you now behold.
What aspiration or inspiration motivated this one to share with
others that which was shared with him or her?

Examine the fibers of the rug beneath your feet. *Feel, touch,
mark similarity and difference.* When you do these things you are
expressing an awareness that leads to greater curiosity, a grander
receptivity and exploration, and—most important—living abundantly, creatively, hopefully, and rewardingly. Beyond this?
Action! Directed action! You are using the creative power of your
mind. Now that you know what you are using and can use, direct
it *forcefully, powerfully, and meaningfully* toward that which you
would have, be, and do. The men who lived long before us did not
know the pattern of the plan. We know what they did with the

images within their minds. They didn't know it all, but they did do something with that with which they had to work.

The creative powers of man's mind, the power to imagine and to direct this image, are the greatest powers man has. The very greatest power man has is—*awareness of God.*

With the power of your mind, and with an awareness of God, what will YOU do with the imaging power of YOUR mind?

WEEKLY PROGRAM
NUMBER

40

The Pattern of an Evolving Power Consciousness

<u>You have tremendous potential within you!</u> This continuing series is structured to release that potential. What you do with the "tools" you already have will determine much that you would have in your life. What will you do? What will you have?

As a human being and a clergyman, I recognize the importance of communication. I realize that all men desire that which will make life more meaningful. I also know there is a way which can and will give meaning. This "way" is a task-master demanding of the seeker. As a clergyman, I am a minister "of sorts" because, knowing that within the frame of reference applied, a minister serves and is diplomatic. At times diplomacy has been discarded in favor of realistic truth and the importance of communication: to disclose, rather than masquerade; reveal rather than conceal; share rather than withold. *You have a tremendous potential within you! What do you do? How do you start? The way to begin is to commence! You have been given the "way." Make a beginning! Take the first step! Start! Act! You do have tremendous potential within you.*

Consistent with this idea is the "pattern of the plan." For every living thing there is a pattern—whether this be an idea within your mind, a hope within your heart, the unexpressed "expression of God" within a small cell, a living, moving human being yet to be—each an image, a pattern of what will be. What idea, image, pattern or plan do you have that you would have come forth into expression?

Every thought you have is consistent with the pattern of the

214

plan you daily and hourly create. What will you do? What will you have? What pattern or plan are you consciously or unconsciously holding to—bringing forth desired or undesired results?

Consider this:

> "Carbon atoms, which have an outer structure consisting of four electrons arranged at the points of a pyramid, build up crystals in several different ways. In one arrangement they form crystals of graphite, which are soft, black, and act as a good lubricant. In another, exactly the same atoms form diamond, brilliant, transparent, and the hardest substance known. Thus the properties of a material depend not only on the atoms of which it is composed, but on the patterns in which they are arranged."
> —George Russell Harrison,"What Man May Be" p. 31.

Thus it is with man and with his mind. The mind with its untold images, ideas, and word pictures, may be compared to a dictionary with its thousands of words, each having importance and meaning, but lacking brilliance and quality until composed and arranged into a pattern of substance.

Intuition is defined as "comprehension without effort." Truth is "conformity of assertion to fact; that which is true." It is a truth that the image you hold in your mind is allied with forces producing success or failure, illness or health, unhappiness or joy. Whatever image is held in the mind is a pattern of the plan, a concept before accomplishment. Knowing this, it would appear simple to "determine" to choose our thoughts and mental images wisely. But wisdom of the mind is incomplete without that which comes as intuition, "comprehension without effort"—God.

YOUR ASSIGNMENT FOR THIS WEEK

The **first factor of proof** is personal experience. So that you can wisely choose images productive of fruitful results, accept these words of scripture: *According to your faith be it unto you."* — *Matthew 9:29. "Commit thy way unto the Lord; trust also in him; and he shall bring it to pass." —Psalm 37:5.*

Read: (Daily) The fourth chapter of the Epistle of Paul to the Ephesians.

After each reading: A time of Silence.

"A time to keep silence, and a time to speak." —Ecclesiastes 3:7

"There was silence, and I heard a voice." —Job 4:16

MAKE THIS—

YOUR DAILY AFFIRMATION FOR THE WEEK:

"I am alive! For this I give grateful thanks. I also know that to be "alive" means to be animated and open to impressions and images to which I respond. I am alive, responsive, responding to the world around me!"

Your basis of reality
in daily living

What does it mean to be alive? The borderline between living and nonliving matter can be stated as simply as the difference between response and vacuity, sentient perceptiveness and insensibility.

What does it mean to be alive? It means that at some time, in some particular area of vital function, there had to be an image, a representation of the form or condition—a mirrored reflection, a counterpart or copy, a likeness or similitude, a picture in the mind, and a pattern of the plan.

To that which I am dead, I am unresponsive. Great works of art, simple things of nature, and profound meanings have no meaning for me unless I respond to the quality of life within them and within me. To a man in a coma, life has little meaning. Life may express itself in a thousand ways around one in a coma, but for this one, life does not exist. For you or me to be unresponsive to the world, opportunity, or spirit causes these things to not exist for us. One who was a physician asked a pertinent question: *"Why seek ye the living among the dead?"* —Luke 24:5. One who wrote a book rich in lessons on conduct and spiritual experiences proclaimed of the God in which he believed, *"A new heart also will I give you, and a new spirit will I put within you."* —*Ezekiel 36:26*

"I am alive! For this I give grateful thanks. I also know that to be "alive" means to be animated and open to impressions and images to which I respond. I am alive, responsive, responding to the world around me!"

In doing that which we have to do we have a responsibility, also a privilege.

Your self-development questions

Question 1. The Ten Commandments of the ancient Hebrews determined for Christians the ethics of good and evil, *absolutely, ultimately, and unquestionably.* Other deep-thinking individuals of integrity have believed that "good" and "evil" are relative to condition, time, and place. Between these diverse perspectives is a question: *How do we reconcile a God that is "all good," and a world filled with much that appears evil, if the world and all that is in it is God-created and supposedly good?*

Question 2. Xenophanes, philosophical poet of the sixth century B.C., bitterly condemned the popular idea that the gods were as mortals: *"Yes, and if oxen or lions had hands and could paint and produce works of art as men do, horses would paint the forms of gods like horses and oxen like oxen. He is a whole, without beginning or ending, and eternal unity. As a whole, God does not move; but his parts do move."* We are told that *God created man in His own image.* Discounting that "man created God in his own (man's) image," allowing limitation of words, *how would you describe God?*

Question 3. *What is YOUR greatest challenge in acceptance of a spiritual principle?*

Question 4. *If I came to you with the above challenge, how would you help me with it?*

"The Lord is my helper, and I will not fear . . ." —Hebrews 13:6

"STIMULATORS TO ACTION"–

As we "dig into" the structure of life, we learn
  that "mastery" of life is only the result of following the
natural rythmn of all
  that has life—the intrinsic, innate, inherent, or essential
quality that is the
  totality of that particular existence.

The flowing of a river,
  waterfall, the force and movement of unseen air, the
silent elevation of tree grown tall—are following poetry, pattern,
and expression, but
  a declaration of meaning, a budding forth—
  bidding forth, explicitly,
  "This is what I was meant to do! To be!"

Your point to query of yourself "What was I meant to do? To
be?"

How to Use Your Understanding Beyond Your Intellect

Others might be tempted to consider a "scientific approach" to that which lies beyond the mind. *There is no "scientific approach" to God or to the deepest of human feelings—love, kindness, and understanding.* There is but one measure of the meaning beyond our ability to verbalize that which is not accessible to words: to discern spiritually. Spiritual means and methods must be utilized, or that which we would perceive will remain imperceptible.

We do not go beyond the intellect with the mind alone—although the mind is a proper starting point, a point of departure toward a destination far unseen and yet unknown.

We speak of God, religion, love, and kindness, and understanding—and none of these qualities of which we speak are obvious or examples of human behavior. On the one hand we appreciate laughter and lightness and the creative inspiration of the poet. We are moved by the sound we call "music." We have an apperception and an appreciation of all that moves us, but we remain "unmoved." We look at clouds and more than eye is lifted aloft. Then the fallibility of man shows itself. For as he directs the eye without, he neither contemplates nor considers that which is within—himself—nor that which he has looked upon. "Untrue," he says of that which is truth itself—and mind decides to go no farther. He will not go beyond the intellect.

Why settle for less

Glorious creature that man can be—he settles for what he isn't. If he would settle for something more, he cannot settle for anything less. Reaching beyond the intellect is not a diversion: there is no wandering of the mind, and no interesting, roundabout pathways along the way. You are on the path and on the way—or .going the wrong way.

YOUR ASSIGNMENT FOR THIS WEEK

Relax! Release! And let go! *Make no attempt to use the mind except as the manner and means of release. Release all thought by thinking this: "I am calm. I am peaceful. I am relaxed."*

And now: Know that you are in the presence of God. Sense, by quiet acceptance, that all around you, no matter what the name—all is God.

Relax! Release! Let go! And let God in!

What is it you would know? What is it you would be? What is it you would do? *Make no attempt to know or be or do. Relax. Release. Let go and let God in.*

And if you question "How?" return once more to your original release: *"I am calm. I am peaceful. I am relaxed."* Words will not suffice, but feeling will.

Repetitious prayers and solicitation may help, but they are not the way or the answer. Their help is but an inclination toward right direction. The right attitude in reaching beyond the intellect lies in these profound and simple words: *"Be still." "Be still, and know that I am God." —Psalm 46:10.*

Accept, believe, and know this truth: *"To be spiritually minded is life and peace." —Romans 8:6*

It is also beyond the intellect.

Again: Know that whatever you would seek and have is a matter of your elevated consciousness, and is beyond the intellect.

Write in your notebook that which you sensed, felt, and knew during your period of silence.

"... now are we the sons of God, and it doth not yet appear what we shall be." —I John 3:2

MAKE THIS—
YOUR DAILY AFFIRMATION FOR THE WEEK:

"Recognizing that my mind is the starting point evoking each act, every thought, and all feeling, I also admit my mind to be that within me which can direct me God-ward. In this, my mind is more than mind—it is beyond the intellect. This day I determine to use the power of my mind to guide me to that power beyond the mind."

Your basis of reality
in daily living

Putting aside the subtleties of the mind we are left with the key to freedom or the means to self-deception. In honesty, we know we function with a power greater than the mind alone. These are the moments of inspiration, creativity, and greatness—and those rare times we truly relate to all and everything. Should we deceive ourselves, we have worshipped mind alone and are self-enclosed in isolation.

Religions, societies, and something within most individuals have been aware of more than a gentle persuasion, employed to impede self-centered activities. Through condemnation, promise, threat, and fear of hell, religion, society, and certain individuals have sought to dissuade themselves and others of the limiting power of consideration of and for the self.

Know this:

"Recognizing that my mind is the starting point evoking each act, every thought, and all feeling, I also admit my mind to be that within me which can direct me God-ward. In this, my mind is more than mind—it is beyond the intellect. This day I determine to use the power of my mind to guide me to that power beyond the mind."

"Ye are this day the stars of heaven for multitude." —Deuteronomy 1:10

Your self-development questions

Question 1. Aristotle propounded an hypothesis "that some men are by nature born slaves and some are by nature born to be free." More than superficially, we see this as a continuum of conceptual thought; i.e., *the power of the mind.* Men do differ from one another in ability, desire, and motivation. Added to this, religion has enslaved masses of men from time immemorial. Discarding all this, *What is the greatest leveler of barriers between men, and how would you apply it?*

Question 2. The statement has been made, "No man is born to be a specific individual in a certain state or stage of life—free or bonded." *Every man IS born to something specific. What is it?* Also, *as his mind keeps him bound or free—how shall he best dispel the mist that clouds his vision and remove "self-forged" shackles?*

Question 3. While it is easily observable that man is a physical being with a mind determining much that affects him and his affairs, the very fact that at times he expresses that which others experience—far beyond what appears to be of the mind or the intellect, makes difficult and debatable any argument that "man's mind alone determines his destiny." *Some will say, "This is God." Others will presume, "This is spirit." What is God and what is spirit?*

Question 4. Young people of today are justifiably disclaimers of Christian ethics. By others than their peers, they are called, among other erroneous denominates, *"Christian radicals."* They are neither Christians nor unbelievers in the accepted sense. They do not ask the question that has been asked, *"Can a truly contemporary person not be an atheist?"* They seek to *know, express, and experience* (other than from a pulpit, or in a book) *Christianity,* as a Man of long ago and far away, knew, expressed, and experienced God. *As one who has been exposed to the doctrine, the dictum, and the theology of a far different presentation, how would you relate meaningfully to the youth of today?*

> **"The wisdom that is from above is first pure, then peaceable, gentle, and easy to be intreated, full of mercy and good fruits, without partiality, and without hypocrisy."** —James 3:17

"STIMULATORS TO ACTION"—

A long time ago—
A gentle, kind, and loving man declared:
"What things soever ye desire, when ye pray, believe that ye

receive them and ye shall have them." —Mark 11:24
When ye pray—believe!
To believe is to give credence to, be persuaded, think to be
true, rely upon, make no doubt of, apprehend, or take.
Determine a worthy desire.
Be persuaded that believing is supereminent
to words or thoughts alone—in spirit!

A QUIET PAUSE BESIDE THE STREAM
OF EVOLVING CONSCIOUSNESS—

By what measure do we determine the measure of a man? What is the yardstick, the measuring rule, by which I determine, not so much what I have been, not so much what I will be, but what I am this very moment?

In this world in which we live, there are many measures by which we predicate the value or the worth of the world around us. We "measure" a field in yards, in acres, or in feet. We "measure" many things by the simple expediency of using rules that are set, established and determined beforehand by bounds within which we must work. We "measure" other things by other standards—by where we stand in relation to a particular person, situation, or condition.

If we were to measure the origin of religion or philosophy, we might say that both "evolved" in the heartbreak of man, in those periods of conflict when he found "self" insufficient, in those moments of despair, he sought for meaning where meaning was but a word. With unprejudiced judgment we could well declare that the "origin of prayer" is through need, while the continuance of prayer is through fulfillment. And with profound consideration we can proclaim that *adherence* to spiritual principles produced individuals of spiritual stature—individuals who resolutely became disciplined to an idea—*disciples of discernment* with the desire to breathe and act and do and be, far beyond the world other men think they see. These disciples of a disciplined life were not concerned with theories, words and rituals, *but with life itself.*

Their conduct had little to do with the past (except as a guideline for the present) less to do with the future (except as a guideline for the present) and everything to do with the present. Their concern was a towering acknowledgment of the present and thus they "presented." themselves daily to observance of order in a world of disorder.

A great effort is required on our part to view them, not as men set apart, but as men whose longing hearts extended beyond longing to a disciplined intent and purpose. For these whose efforts set them apart there was no abstract formula. A definite, positive, intelligible, comprehensible purpose determined their life: *To know God and to be one with their fellow man.* If you never read another line, if you never hear another message in your life, if you never have another admonition presented to you—never forget this:

> "I have but one purpose in my life that will measure me as I evolve, give stature that I might see, and in finding, give worth, quality, meaning and determination to my life and to the lives of those with whom I come in contact—one thing alone, my purpose: To know God and to be one with my fellow man."

There will never be a pearl of greater wisdom than this thoughtful, disciplined purpose: *To know God and to be one with my fellow man.*

There are no subtle psychological distinctions. *"I have set before you life and death, blessing and cursing; choose ye!"* If we are to measure our lives, by what do we measure? By what deed? By what discipline? The discipline of a disciple? The "attempt" to know God and be one with our fellow man? By what means do we measure our life? By words? *Or by disciplined deeds? Each a disciple!*

How to Be an Effective
Follower for Daily Benefits

To discipline ourselves around regular programs is a unique challenge for most of us. While the definition of "discipline" is "obedience to rules," for our purpose we can say that "discipline" is to "apprehend the truth of being; to lay hold of with understanding" and to "discriminate;" i.e.: "to distinguish intelligently and to choose the desirable."

Theories are fine, but to have meaning, they must prove applicable. We reconcile theory or principle only through application. The first step in our discipline is to know what it is that we aspire to.

YOUR ASSIGNMENT FOR THIS WEEK

The discipline begins. Divine discontent is the ground upon which we stand and a starting point to an evolving consciousness. *Spiritually, what is it you would attain? Write it down in your notebook after prayerful consideration.*

Understanding of self begins with inquiry into the nature and relation of things.

After prayerful consideration, write down in your notebook that which you relate to the least. Make a point of understanding and relating to it.

Now: Read and digest every word in the third chapter of the book of Ecclesiastes. Do this daily for the remainder of the week. This book is discipline for the disciple and a revelation for the discipline.

"Whosoever will, let him take the water of life freely." —Revelations 22:17

MAKE THIS—

YOUR DAILY AFFIRMATION FOR THE WEEK:

"I am an instrument in the hands of God—for my hands are God's hands and my mind is the mind of God. My every act and thought express the character and quality of a divine being!"

Your basis of reality in daily living

All great religions, philosophies, and insights have their origin through the minds, lives, and actions of those who recognized the greatness of all men and the relationship of all, without separation or distinction. These individuals knew and know that God is the living substance of the only reality they will ever know. In its most positive connotation, this "reality" becomes a discipline and the individual a disciple. There is no equating God with an unknown principle.

The everlasting cry of humanity is to find "truth," meaning and purpose. This will never be found in the cleverness of the mind. It is to be found only in the humility discovered in affinity. *This is a discipline. You are the disciple.*

"I am an instrument in the hands of God—for my hands are God's hands and my mind is the mind of God. My every act and thought express the character and quality of a divine being!"

Your self-development questions

Question 1. Of the twelve disciples (Apostles) chosen by Jesus, most were simple, unlearned men. Each had a profound effect on the lives of countless men and women. *What quality of character did each (including Judas Iscariot) have that we would benefit by having?*

Question 2. Religion should have as a goal right relation between man and God, man and man, and man and nature. This immortal relationship is in perfect conformity with reason and knowledge. *In vast areas, religion, and the church have failed in this. Why?*

Question 3. "Truth" is a name, given by seekers of truth to anything that proves to be good, valid, and of worth. *Assuming that "the spiritual life" is "good, valid, and of worth" and that you have not proven this in your own life by application of principles, what would move you to test the principle fully?*

Question 4. In the pursuit of the material necessities of life, man exhausts and depletes himself. There lies before him a door, waiting to be opened, to a life that is vital and universal and available to him. This requires of him a discipline and that he become a disciple. The path is prayer, meditation, and silence. *Will you determine to set aside a time, proving principle and practice? If you will, state your reasons why you believe this will be helpful to you.* If you are interested, contact the author, through the publisher, regarding your participation in a group for prayer, meditation, and the practice of the Silence.

> **"Approving ourselves as the ministers of God, . . . By pureness, by knowledge, . . . by kindness, . . . by love unfeigned."–II Corinthians 6:4,6.**

"STIMULATORS TO ACTION"–

> *Become still!*
> *In stillness you have*
> *turned to a higher source of inspiration,*
> *Strength and motivation–*
> *Beyond reason and intellect–*
> *You will be moved!*
> *"Let judgment run down as waters, and righteousness as a mighty stream."*
>
> *–Amos 5:24*

WEEKLY PROGRAM
NUMBER
43

How to Unfold
Your Inner Power

Every sensible individual seeks freedom of thought and the right to pursue the religion or philosophy of his own choosing. This very freedom has too often brought absurdity and false reward. Freedom to choose demands discipline to discern.

Unfolding your inner powers means a change in outer conditions, circumstances, and relationships. Inner unfoldment means awareness of self and others, and the expression of potential in performance. Performance requires discipline. It is incomprehensible that one seeking greater meaning in his life would continue as an observer and not as a participant. Philosophy, seeking, searching, religion, meaning, and understanding—inner unfoldment—*require a uniting with that which is sought.*

To grow and unfold, to know God and fellow man, and to relate with meaning to this world of which we are so very much a part, requires no long theological dissertation, imponderable tenet, or mystic ritual—only the simplicity of an earnest desire, a discipline oriented toward bird and tree, mountain stream and wind upon the sea, and an awareness of more than our fears and our desires. Only when the mind and heart contain no outer reservation is there inner revelation. Only then do we unfold, develop, and display that we have unraveled that which only we have declared "unclear."

There is truth in all religion. Unswerving direction in every philosophy. Whatever gulf we encounter between seeking and discovery rests within desire, discipline, and discernment—and the freedom we exercise short of fulfillment. We are free to choose,

228

seek, discuss, and intellectualize. We are bound and bonded to the results of our own choosing. Unfoldment comes through firsthand experience. The great and good persons whose lives we read about *lived the lives we read about.* Theirs was no second-hand religion, watered-down philosophy, superficial speculating, or a vow to be "this" instead of "that." Theirs was a capability without pattern or form—a sensitive receptivity to the world in which they lived.

To realize the highest form of unfoldment of inner power is to recognize neither choice nor determination, but the pursuit of a continuing awareness, for life, to unfold, must encompass, embrace, and relate. Life is not a passive awareness, but a pliable acuity.

YOUR ASSIGNMENT FOR THIS WEEK

Up until this moment substitution may have, for you, been a matter of value. You may have settled for less than you sought. Examining the steps outlined here and Disciplines 7 and 21, you are now stepping out in the direction of self-discovery. You recognize the importance of guidance, but are now also aware of the greater importance of the experience of self-realization. You know the importance of another pointing the way. If you are progressing, you are perceptive that it is <u>you</u> who must do the work, exercise the discipline, and reap the reward.

Preparation: Practice breathing as outlined in the seventh week's program scene: You are in a quiet valley, lying on your back, surrounded by towering mountains. Overhead, clouds drift slowly by. Tall pines upon the slopes scent the air you breathe. Relax and give thought to only this moment—you have freed your mind of all else that would distract.

Now: Select and impress deeply upon your mind the cloud, a tree, or the mountain peak—just one—and nothing else. Let this part of nature become your nature. Peace—beauty—life—you and it—are one.

Set aside a time and place each day and practice the way of a pilgrim upon the path.

In a notebook make note of the changes within yourself.

"Is not this the fast that I have chosen? . . . to let the oppressed go free, and that ye break every yoke?" —Isaiah 58:6

MAKE THIS—

YOUR DAILY AFFIRMATION FOR THE WEEK:

"I seek but one thing: inner unfoldment. Though the means and method may vary, my purpose and intent must always embrace one direction—inner unfoldment and awareness of God."

You basis of reality in today's living

Symbolism is a search for identification. Indigenous and basic to the need and nature of the human being are the symbols he creates to represent deeper forms of expression. Symbols express what we think and to some extent what we desire. Eminently more noticeable than the symbol we create is that which we symbolize—that which we are—not only in mind, but in body and affairs also. Symbols are mere representations. Desire transforms potential into expression and meaning into experience.

"I seek but one thing: inner unfoldment. Though the means and method may vary, my purpose and intent must always embrace one direction—inner unfoldment and awareness of God."

The development of a man, a mind, and a purpose—

There is a strange paradox in the mind of man. He seeks, shifts and shuttles back and forth. The energy he expends on wasted effort could bring a world of rich reward. The questions are before you. The answers lie within.

Your self-development questions

Question 1. As we seek to achieve the vital sense of possibility—an awareness that life can be shaped to a purpose—we are faced with a twofold intent. If we would live a meaningful life, *we must know God.* If we would know God, *we must live a meaningful life. Rephrase this statement so that it will "re-phase" your life.*

Question 2. Each new experience is a door we approach allowing part of ourself to step forth and open wide or close tightly. Behind each door lies all possibilities: refusal, darkness, suspicion, fear— and joy, happiness, and sharing. Behind the door may be darkness. We can bring light. *How can we approach each door so that regardless of what we find on the other side, it will prove of value to all concerned?*

Question 3. There is but one purpose in knowing God, and that is in *knowing* God. *What does the foregoing mean to you?*

Question 4. We can find God in all places, persons, and things. *How can we arrive at a constant awareness of God's constant presence?*

Formulate a question you would like answered. *Present it to another to answer.*

"By his knowledge the depths are broken up, and the clouds drop down the dew."

                                                    —Proverbs 3:20

"STIMULATORS TO ACTION"—

*All our efforts for growth, understanding, and
betterment must be preceded by an awareness that whatever
we want allows no room for doubt or inactivity.
Our mind, body, being,
and spirit must be saturated intensely
with the desire for growth, understanding, and betterment,
and we must act in accord with this desire.*

Whatever your desire, grasp it: get excited about it. Make it part of your every thought. Let it become your prayer. Act upon it. Think of the many ways in which you can relate it to your every activity. Growth, understanding, and betterment are your every activity.

WEEKLY PROGRAM NUMBER

44

How to Tear Down the Negative Walls You've Built Around Yourself

We do not see the air we breathe, nor do we see the strength of character within an individual sustaining him and others—but they are there. There are walls of strength and spirit, though they may not be visible to the casual eye, and there are walls of separation that sever and separate, keeping others from us and keeping us from greater good. All of these are within the mind, projected from the spirit of what we fail to feel.

We think that we "feel," and this is why we are the way we are. But is this really so? Wherever there is strength there is always awareness, knowledge, concern, and understanding. The abrasiveness of separation, the "wall" within our mind, is due to failure to detect beyond the surface and comprehend that which appears distant to ourselves—and thus we build a wall, not encompassing others within that which is a strength to us, but keeping others out and our good beyond the wall we've built.

In pondering these thoughts, brevity is bound to make for oversimplification. But a deeper consideration of these thoughts will prove either an indictment or an inducement. The choice is ours. We have the material to work with. We are the master builders. The purpose, function, and design are of our doing. If we build alone, we go too far—*alone*. Build with God (or call it what you will) and we will not miss the significant comprehension that you and I are more than creatures seeking "self" alone. We are mutual in attachment and reciprocal in responsibilities. What we exemplify in our own life—can it be recommended to others? We are justified in doing that which dignifies, and razes walls of abasement, large or small. There is profound reason for building that which encompasses God and fellow man. We become a compelling influence for good in the lives of others and a recipient of the good we seek for ourselves.

What shall we build and how? A life without limit—through a power greater than the individual self. I call this power "God."

YOUR ASSIGNMENT FOR THIS WEEK

For this project of the mind and spirit, we need no blueprint, plan, site. We need few thoughts determining our construction except those which will come forth in quiet meditation.

The preparation:

As those who look upon the stars know them through observation and interest, you who would know God, meaning, and fellow man—ultimately self—must, through interest, attitude, action, and quiet meditation, acquaint yourself with what you seek.

In quiet contemplation: With every thought that comes to mind, consider that which is Godlike about it. God is here, there, and everywhere. Stand beside a river, lake, or rumbling waterfall. Is this water and nothing more? Love, inspiration, sharing, doing, and being—are these but words? What are these things? What and who is your neighbor but you—across the street—or side by side? Need we ask the question? More likely we need to contemplate.

Dwell upon each thought, person, place, circumstance that comes to mind. Know that God is in what you behold. *"Acquaint now thyself with him, and be at peace." —Job 22:21. "That thou mayest walk in the way of good men, and keep the paths of the righteous." —Proverbs 2:20. "As the branch cannot bear fruit of itself, except it abide in the vine; no more can ye, except ye abide in me" —John 15:4. "If therefore thine eye be single, thy whole body shall be full of light." —Matthew 6:22*

MAKE THIS—

YOUR DAILY AFFIRMATION FOR THE WEEK:

"I determine this day, in a new awareness, to be loving and kind, and to make myself an influence for good—in all things, in all ways, and at all times."

Your basis of reality in today's living

How abundantly clear it should be that love, kindness and consideration promote in kind that which we have extended. Yet for some, this would not be a statement of clarity. For though clarity means awareness, there is much in the lives of many that is obscured which can be brought into focus by kindness and consideration.

Awareness, while not the exclusive faculty of man, is his to express in ways given to none other. He alone can resolve a thousand different sorrows into a thousand different joys through awareness of the meaning of kindness and consideration. Kindess, consideration, and love show awareness of the world in which we live.

To truly live is to know ourselves and our relationship with others, not only as a world of close associates, ideas, and personal possessions, but extending—from man to nature—through our God-given capacity to love.

"I determine this day, in a new awareness, to be loving and kind, and to make myself an influence for good—in all things, in all ways, and at all times."

Like a chip upon the wave—

How often we are as "the chip upon the wave." We toss to and fro without really getting anywhere. There is a lot of movement with little progress. When we decide to "take the bull by the horns," "both oars in our hands," and determine a course of action, we are already on our way.

Your self-development questions

Question 1. We "perceive" what we "perceive"—but that which we "perceive" may not be that which *is perceived!* Confused? The practical consequence of seeing anything for what it is results in a relationship beyond conceptual determination of an attitude based on appearance. Concept formation posits relationships based on theory rather than on designative significance. *How would you determine right observation and, consequently, right understanding?*

Question 2. Much of the difficulty in human relations can be directly attributed to failure to communicate. To a great degree, the murkiness of misunderstanding proceeds from unclear images within the mind resulting from inability to express what one thinks one knows. *There is a way of removing this wall separating man from man, other than the ability to articulate persuasively. What is it?*

Question 3. Since we seem to structure our attitudes and actions on signs that function as designators of attitude and action, how then do we *go beyond the physical indicator to the subtler verity that merges rather than separates?*

Question 4. A word upon the printed page is but a squiggle of ink—unless and until we give it meaning. Even then it may have meaning without our understanding. The tone of the voice, the tilt and turn of the head, and the expression on the face all convey meaning. Everything we say, or do or think is denotative and connotative of a particular. *Some of us have learned to "read the signs." None of us can say we are without knowledge gained from observation. One wonders why, when we really know that others are very much like us, there should be the great chasm of misunderstanding. Your thoughts?*

> **"The man that wandereth out of the way of understanding shall remain in the congregation of the dead." —Proverbs 21:16**

"STIMULATORS TO ACTION"–

Open your Bible at random.
   Let your eyes wander, without effort,
  across the open pages.
      Somewhere—where you have gazed—
      Something will stand out.
Take this inspired thought, grasp it and hold it deep within, and as you "grasp" it will give meaning, across time and eternity, stimulating to action that which "stimulated to action"—another man, another mind!

45

The Power of a Time of Silence

The importance of a time for silence

This may be a matter of supreme indifference to the average individual hurrying to and fro in an effort to consummate effort with results—to earn a living; to attain happiness; to know what to do with time of which he has less and less.

But it is important for the rare and fortunate individual who recognizes the importance of a time of Silence, who admits the importance of renewal and realization beyond speculation. *It is for this one, or two, or more, that these words are spoken—for whom the ear, no longer deaf, shall hear the sound of God, and whose eyes, no longer blind, shall see the constant vision of God and good.*

For those of you who would attune the listening ear—
A Time of Silence!

Silence—what a wonderful word! *But for many it is totally without meaning.* In a world of clamor and constant sound, "silence" is a word without meaning. Should you ask, "What is silence?" the answer would be, *"A quiet time of conversation with God" wherein you hear that with no sound.* The whole substance of religion, faith, hope, trust, love, understanding, and relatedness issued forth in the stillness of quiet consideration, reflection of values and contemplation of meaning.

Only in times of stillness does the flower grow, the spirit rise, the mind conceive, and man beget his divine inheritance. In calm repose God talks, and the open heart listens to more than ear can hear.

"*A Time of Silence!*"–and all the world attunes to the intimate presence: one with thee, and me, and you and I, and he, and she–*one!*

Would you speak to God and would that God would speak with you? *Speak out! Whatever words your heart would say–say!* And then, serene, you'll find no words to match the words your heart receives–and you suppress the verbal sound and speak more loudly than heretofore: *"This is 'a time of Silence!' "* You hear *thoughts you know are more than thought, for this is your quiet time of conversation with God.*

> **"Thou hast hid these things from the wise and prudent, and hast revealed them unto babes." –Matthew 11:25**

Most of us have a set time to get up and retire. We eat at certain hours and perform certain rituals of life with regularity. Things of God, of spirit, and of spiritual discipline–our life, time, interest, and results–are pretty much a hit-or-miss affair. Diligence of interest up to this time will have proved the importance of discipline.

Perhaps you are aware that these programs (disciplines) are primarily devoted to the practice of prayer, the Silence, and meditation. A gentle reminder: Set aside a few minutes each day to be quiet–a time in which you refrain from conversation, reading, and, as much as possible, from thinking random, uncontrolled, undirected thoughts. This will be preparation for that which is to follow.

YOUR ASSIGNMENT FOR THIS WEEK

Determine and set a time of silence. Adhere to this schedule you have resolved. Make a genuine effort to remain completely quiet during this time and observe this time.

Form a habit of prefacing this time with a few words of silent prayer.

As you continue and progress with the forthcoming series of disciplines, you will thrill to discover your time of prayer little different from other times of the day, for gradually, your conversation will be with God—under all circumstances and at all times.

Now: In your notebook, determine both the prayer you will use and the time of day you set aside.

"Beloved, now are we the sons of God, and it doth not yet appear what we shall be: but we know that, when he shall appear, we shall be like him." —1 John 3:2

MAKE THIS—

YOUR DAILY AFFIRMATION FOR THE WEEK:

"From this moment forward I set aside a few moments each day to quiet my mind. Briefly I contemplate all for which I can give thanks. And then, in stillness, I listen to the "still small voice within." The voice I would hear when I would hear the voice of God.

Your basis of reality in today's living

Silence is more than absence of sound. Silence is receptivity to that which must be spiritually discerned. Silence *is* attunement with that beyond the limit of what we hear with physical ears.

"The Silence," in its totality, is not death, but the vibrancy of life. Silence is a river crossed, a mountain climbed, a problem solved. Silence is the closing out of a world, but an opening of the universe. It is knowing rather than wondering; finding, rather than seeking. It is ultimate recognition that prayer, silence, devotion, giving, sharing, being, and doing include the whole of life. Man's oblation its own reward in the time of Silence!

"I contemplate all for which I can give thanks. And then, in stillness, I listen to "the still small voice."

Your self-development questions

Question 1. Regardless of or by whatever name we call religion, gymnastics of the mind, or seeking of the soul for spirit—there is, in actuality, but one substance we are seeking: God—in our lives, our affairs, and our consciousness. One would be well advised that knowing God is neither mysterious nor obscure. *List several ways in which you can, in a very practical way, express God in relation to others.*

Question 2. Many suggestions and procedures have been presented for finding God. A specific procedure is through the Silence. *What has at least one spiritual teacher, including Jesus, had to say regarding entering the Silence?*

Question 3. Ideas are always in conflict. You and I want something. Are we willing to do that which must be done to receive it? It has been said, "When a man has plowed and sweated over a field, he feels quite differently about it than about a chance sand dune." *Are you willing to make a commitment and a covenant with God?* If your answer is yes, write: *My covenant with God is to devote at least fifteen minutes each day, quietly and in silence."*

Question 4. Silence is a powerful step toward God. However there are times when it is far removed from anything Godlike; i.e., a word of appreciation left unsaid; that which we have taken for granted; the time when we must stand up and be counted—and we have remained silent. This question must be answered within your own heart: *What can I do or say that only through me will spiritually enrich?*

> **"Render therefore to all their dues: . . , honour to whom honor."**
> —Romans 13:7

"STIMULATORS TO ACTION"—

The first step
In the right direction
Toward a better life
Is:
A good impression of yourself,
a better opinion of your fellowman
And the faith in God to prove both the impression and opinion.

Mindful of the importance religion and the church can have in your life—*a thought about religion, the church, you and me: Religion shall not be found in a book, a room, or an edifice.*

Limitless possibilities
you can open for yourself

Much has been said today of the failure of religion: the failure of churches and clergymen to realistically meet the needs of the times in which we live. There is most certainly a truth to this.

Most clergymen fail to speak out on issues vital and relative to the deepest concerns of men and women in and out of church. They are not entirely to blame for their hesitancy, for not a few have paid the high price of standing up for that they believe in, and standing out as a clear representation of what they know. In a broader sense all of us pay a very high price *for an unwillingness to stand up and be counted.*

If someone asked "How are you?" how many would be willing to stand up and say, "I am strong in the power of the Lord!"— either in words or in silence? *And how many would know what this means in health, life, love, and animation?*

The spirit which gave birth, life, and animation to Christianity shaped the lives of a few men and became the character of a thousand symbols—all in the name of God, but few having anything to do with either God or man. What could have become a rising tide of good in the lives of men—dynamic and powerful— weakened and ebbed away. In its wake was left symbols representing far less than the real thing.

What have we done with the most magnificent truths of the greatest teachers of all time? We speak of love, life, and living—and we neither love nor live. We speak of finding "the law of life," and disregard the rules for living. *We have a role as well as a goal.*

We set aside a piece of land and build a place of worship wherein we can gather together one with another. It is a monument to what we would not seek. We worship the sanctity of a building built by hands; *and sacrifice the creation of that created by God.* There is no inherent sanctity in a building, word, or ritual. *There is a sanctity in how much we love life, truth, meaning, purpose, and our fellow man.*

In every area of life we live in a world of our own making. We speak of "God-likeness," and see it neither in ourselves nor in others. We look to the symbols we have created and see that there is no end to the worship of the self and adulation and adoration of all that is symbolic. We would be aghast were one to use the Bible as a footstool—*but we use our fellow man as a "stepping stone."* We say, "The Bible is the word of God!" *The Bible is a book printed for a profit, little more than ink upon a page—unless and until it is lived. Then it is the Word of God, the inspiration and motivation of meaning in your life and mine.* Human life is holier than the scripture we quote, and human life can have a grandeur to it more magnificent than the greatest cathedral. But never so long as we take direction for granted, appearance for principle, and a casual interest for practice.

For most human beings, the lives they live, the efforts they make, and the rewards they reap are little more than a commentary on the message of Jesus, Krishna, Sri Ramakrishna Buddha. We make a mystery out of that which is neither mysterious nor difficult to understand, and in a very real sense, we make a mockery of that which could give meaning. We have the principles for a better life and a better world. We must apply them.

We say the church has failed; this is true. We observe that religion has little meaning; there is much to validate this observation. We contend that opportunities for spiritual development do not exist in a church, a religion, or in the world in which we live. It is always possible for a church, a religion, a philosophy, our life, and the world in which we live to falter, fail, and crumble. As many opportunities exist for you, me, the church, our religion, our philosophy, the world in which we live, and our lives to be the magnificent example we would have it be—*if we would have it be!*

What is this church that has so miserably failed? This church is people—not buildings, projects and altars, but the sanctuary within your heart and mine, and a willingness to stand up and be counted as a living representation of the teachings of Jesus Christ. *"Love ye one another." "Wilt thou be made whole?" "That which I have done—ye can do also—and even greater things!"* And this religion of so little meaning? Religion shall not be found in a book, a room, or an edifice. Religion is deep within the heart, soul, mind, body, spirit, and affairs of one very real human being *relating to another—and another—and another—and to all there is in this world in which we live—and thus to the spirit of God.*

What is religion? It is a moment of joy and happiness, a time of sorrow, trial, tribulation, understanding, and compassion, *and the ability to know that others feel as you do, though they mask it in a thousand ways.* And the "nonexistent opportunities" for spiritual development?

All of us genuinely want and desire a better and more meaningful life. We get lost somewhere between desire and action. If we are the church, what can we do about the religion or philosophy about which we recognize much that *is* wrong? We can stop waiting for the other person to finish talking so that we can have our own say. We can listen instead of trying to be heard—and others will hear what we don't have the words to say. We can apply the principles given in a thousand ways by a thousand whose lives were the example.

Love, activity, and participation are the tests of meaning—extending far beyond the words we use to an extension of the God we say we believe in. Can I meet your needs? Can you meet mine? *No!* But I can listen to your heart, and you can listen to the spirit of mine. The sound we hear will be the voice of God.

WEEKLY PROGRAM
NUMBER
46

How to Know Your Limitless Possibilities

One who is truly capable of thinking must comprehend that life extends beyond the narrow confines within which most men live. In moments of awareness, most men glimpse a knowing transcending uncertainty—and then, as shifting sands, heedless of that which has been given, drift into inaction, as footprints upon the sand.

In the profoundest sense, one truly capable of thinking insists upon a reason for his existence. In his ultimate maturity he knows that life is more than paradox—he determines life's limitless possibilities. In this determination, in this awareness of animation, he who thinks, ponders, reflects, contemplates, and meditates, comprehends life's limitless possibilities for growth and understanding—or inactivity and self-deceit.

Unless we understand that whatever we expect, demand, wish for, or desire from others, or from things—is also required of us in some way, we limit possibilities, but only in that which we would have—for endless are the possibilities of that which we would not have.

Limitless possibilities! Such is the condition and the reality of your mind and mine. There is no end to growth. We cannot live by illusion; there is only existence. However there is reality behind whatever the illusion: this is the saving grace.

An alteration of point of view—an application of principles—will simultaneously dissolve disorder in your life and enable you to not only be an actor on a stage, but to observe and participate much more fully in life. This should be the ultimate aim of one with desire for an evolving consciousness. The possibilities are unlimited.

YOUR ASSIGNMENT FOR THIS WEEK

The following exercise is twofold in purpose: 1.) To resolve potential into performance, and 2.) In this resolve—relate!—to God and fellow man.

Determine to be diligent—to pursue through performance to results. Prior to your time of concentration, observe your immediate surroundings. That which is both disturbing or distressing, and pleasant—*release.* Accept them both from a different perspective. Regard both in an attitude of calm serenity without either distress or joy. Impersonally, without distraction, you now proceed to:

The discipline: The character of what you will now experience will depend upon how willingly you embrace the discipline itself. Your growth and evolvement are neither accidental nor dependent upon someone else. It is your choice and your determination.

Paradoxically, that which we seek requires that we already have that which is sought. Important to a deepening experience of health, abundance, and the ability to meditate is a healthy condition of mind and body. This begins within the mind.

As you prepare for contemplative meditation, hold to the thought of health for yourself in mind, body, and affairs. Do more than "think" this. *Believe; affirm health and order in all things concerning you.*

Relax! Breathe deeply! Sit with back erect, feet upon the floor, hands in lap. For a moment, seek that which is God-like in every thought you have. *Now:* think no thought. Let God come to you in this moment of quietness. In activity, God will be with you—*in all things.*

Observe the above as a daily discipline.

"So then faith cometh by hearing, and hearing by the word of God!" —Romans 10:11

MAKE THIS—

YOUR DAILY AFFIRMATION FOR THE WEEK:

"I will, each day, and in every moment, do the best I can to develop my mind, expand the expression of spirit in my affairs, and live as I would that others would live with me."

Your basis of reality
in today's living

There can be no doubt about the tremendous impact certain individuals make on life and all with whom they come in contact. Theirs is a living example of the truth other men talk about. It is not by fate nor fortune that they are representative of the meaning we seek. They have set themselves resolutely and responsibly to a pattern and a path of their own choice. It is unmistakably clear to them that awareness cannot be gained by continued acceptance of ideas without ideation or desire without disturbance of insentience.

Nothing representative of the meaning you seek demands stratification or slavery to a life of less than meaning. Nothing is clearer than the observation that you were meant to be more than most men ever become. You are a capable creature. Insight is yours if you wish.

"I will, each day, and in every moment, do the best I can to develop my mind, expand the expression of spirit in my affairs, and live as I would that others would live with me."

Are you a "first-rate
second-hand man?"

Are you a person in a world with a fence around it which you can't get over? If you are, let's face facts realistically. Life is very much like riding a bicycle: either you move or you fall off. If you stand still, the world moves on without you.

Unless you have specific spiritually oriented goals, you are working by guess, and you haven't a prayer of a chance.

The material presented is for the improvement of your life and affairs. The rewards are rich and abundant—*if you are willing to apply them.*

Your self-development questions

Question 1. Charles Fillmore, in *The Revealing Word*, defines meditation as "continuous and contemplative thought; to dwell mentally on anything; realizing the reality of the Absolute; a steady effort of the mind to know God; man's spiritual approach to God." He further states: "The purpose of meditation is to expand the consciousness Christward; to bring into realization divine Truth; to be transformed in spirit, soul, and body by the renewing of the mind." *While this is true, and a great many individuals dwell on varied things, many do not seem to find that which they hold within the mind. Why?*

Question 2. It has been declared that everything exists within the mind before it exists in the world in any form. In opposition to this tenet it can be said that one can see things outside of oneself which, until the moment of observation, most certainly were not within the mind. *The difference between perceiving and conceiving is considerable. If both statements are true—and they are—how do you reconcile them?*

Question 3. The most plausible argument is the one that has succeeded in persuading us to accept a premise presented. George Berkeley, whose first important work, *Essay towards a New Theory of Vision,* appeared in 1709, presents us with a challenging premise concerning *the principles of human knowledge*: "The plainest things in the world, those we are most intimately acquainted with, and perfectly know, when they are considered in an abstract way, appear strangely difficult and incomprehensible." *How can anything which we "know" and with which we are familiar become "strangely difficult and incomprehensible" when we develop greater awareness of it?*

Question 4. Most certainly our original concept of God did not originate within the self. Exposure to family preference, persuasion, prejudice, social structure, the mirroring of the minds of other men, individual acceptance or rejection, and comprehensibility all admittedly are part of and an extension of this inconsistent concept. *Spiritual substance either exists or it does not. How can you properly "know" so that you are transformed in spirit, soul, and body? Meditate upon your answer and then share your observation with another.*

"Thou art not far from the kingdom of God." —Mark 12:34

"STIMULATORS TO ACTION"—

Consider that in which you have an interest.
Interest already demands attention.
Look at the world in your immediate vicinity.
   There is much about every part of this world of yours
     that is interesting, exciting, and ennobling.
   Choose one facet
   Observe it closely.
Considered observation results in intensive interest.
   Interest—stimulation—action are
     One and the same!

WEEKLY PROGRAM
NUMBER
47

How to Find Practical
Harmony in Daily Living

A musician worthy of the name knows that much has been demanded of him. For him to render melodious tones pleasing to the ear, discipline and the fulfillment of demand must modify intent into purpose and expression.

From every aspirant of the spirit a few sometimes difficult conditions must be met. The results of spiritual discipline enable you and me to go beyond rule and ritual to the basic structure of the meaning of religion to unalterable truths of spiritual realization. We do this only as we accept the discipline: there is no other way. So long as faith is but a wish, it cannot be a reality. Something is demanded of us. In our wishful piety we are contemptuous of the truth we claim we seek.

Tolstoy observed "That so long as the inexorable spectacle of death and misery, the evanescent drama of life and creation, the overwhelming awareness of want and insignificance of human life remains, man will continue to have religion." To relegate religion (the spiritual quest) to less than the first and most important consideration in life is to discard values that have given man the only way to comprehension of himself, love for his fellow man, a sense of ethical and moral values, and a means to determine life meaningfully for himself and others.

In this day of speculation about the importance of religion and that which churches have presented, no one has ushered in a principle approximating promise. Whatever the failure of that which has been spiritually given, each one must ask himself: *"Have I applied the principles?"* If one has, after application, found barren results, that one most definitely is entitled to question, and to seek elsewhere.

In human relations, the rendition of a song, the expression of all that is good, and beautiful, equate with the harmony of a soul who has sought. The entire issue boils down to this one vital question: *"Have I sought? Have I really applied the principles?"* Anyone can ask the question: only you know the answer. What have you done? What will you do?

YOUR ASSIGNMENT FOR THIS WEEK

If you seek for God, harmony in your life, or good in any form, it must embrace the well-being of all. We know that we cannot change the world. But we can change ourselves and our attitudes toward others, respecting the limitations of others and the byproducts of these limitations. The first step and the most vital principle in the harmonizing of your life and affairs, actively giving power and energy to all you do, is to combine with your total personality a deeper regard for all things.

Again, as notes, bars, and scales of music must be rhythmic and harmonious to be free from dissonance, so also your religion and your life must undergo the discipline of renovation to be orderly, powerful and effective.

The supreme aim: *Unfoldment for Inner Power*

Procedure: In all things reduce the "I." From this day forward, consider the many ways in which *you* can see in others and in all things that which declares: *"You and I are one."*

Now: Disappointment is not born of realization. *Expect to realize the fruits of your efforts.* Your experience will be one with that of kindred spirits, the music of the soul satisfying the desire of the heart.

Make note of that which you have received.

" . . . not as the word of men, but as it is in truth, the word of God." —I Thessalonians 2:13

MAKE THIS—

YOUR DAILY AFFIRMATION FOR THE WEEK:

"There is a truth that can set me free. That truth is the harmony of the soul. I enter into life with anticipation this day. That which I will experience is the fulfillment of that which I hold within my mind. I give grateful thanks that the music of the soul is a harmony chosen by me."

Your basis of reality in daily living

In answer to a query as to how he advanced spiritually, Epictetus replied, "In every circumstance I will keep my will in harmony with nature. To whom belongs that will? To Him in whom I exist."

Everything is either in a state of rhythm or in dissonant discord—your life and mine, the air we breath, rocks and rills and mountain streams. All follow a pattern indicating order and harmony, or disruption; a uniting, or a dispersion. Many things in nature determine the condition of that which is affected. You and I alone determine the harmony of the self, the music of the soul.

"There is a truth that can set me free. That truth is the harmony of the soul. I enter into life with anticipation this day. That which I hold within my mind. I give grateful thanks that the music of the soul is a harmony chosen by me."

Step by step—

We have traveled upon a path of our own making. We tend to take the credit—but only when there is success. We do not fail to blame others, conditions, circumstances, time, place, or events for whatever befalls, hindering us upon our path. We rightfully can take credit for what we have achieved.

Your self-development questions

Question 1. Man's adventure in the realm of free thought and spiritual quest is too often terminated by the obvious and visible world. He finds himself confronted with experiences he allows to impede him; he submits to the tyranny of outside forces. *In an effort to resolve what appears unresolvable, not only what can, but what must one do to realize the harmony that is "the music of the soul"?*

Question 2. Bishop Fulton J. Sheen observed, "The modern soul has definitely limited its horizon; having negated the eternal destinies, it has lost its trust in nature. . . . Man now finds that he is locked up within himself, his own prisoner." *—Peace of Soul,* pp. 2-3. Thus the stream of his own consciousness has brought disharmony to that which could be consistent with peace, amity, *friendship, kind feeling, and understanding. How best would you renew the trust entrusted unto you?*

Question 3. Eric S. Waterhouse, discussing in his book, *The Philosophical Approach to Religion,* various perspectives concerning definitions of religion, ventures that "Religion is man's attempt to supplement his felt insufficiency by allying himself with a higher order of being which he believes is manifest in the world and can be brought into sympathetic relationship with himself, if rightly approached."*How do we justify the faith in the values discussed?*

Question 4. Srimat Puragra Parampanthi made this profound statement: "Self-denial, renunciation, spiritual exercise, codes of ethics, worship, prayer, philosophy, aesthetics *are not religion [italics mine].* They have relation to religion only in so far as they assist . . . [the] person to attain the highest goal: harmony of soul with the Supreme Being or Order. Religion is unique, specific expression and it cannot be equated with anything. It finds its own vindication in religious experiences." *Presuming the foregoing to be a basic truth, how does one have religious experiences?*

"Mary said, My soul doth magnify the lord." —Luke 1:46

"STIMULATORS TO ACTION"—

How necessary is the air you breathe?
More than important—absolute and essential.
*Frame and fashion, form and shape, whatever you would
have—In a context just as real.*
Lax and torpid one—you will be moved!

WEEKLY PROGRAM

NUMBER

48

How to Benefit from Your Experience

The poet, wishing to magnify that which has magnified him, extols the virtue of life around him, the world in which he lives, and thus the world in which he lives becomes a living, vibrant, part of all he is—and only a small part of that of which he writes. He dreams big dreams and envisions beyond the field of vision to a purer perceptual awareness. He knows he is part of all and all is part of him.

Looking beyond external signs he apprehends himself not a mendicant but a co-creator with that which created him. He perceives that *all* he looks upon is also within. In the confused and restless world the poet detects the mark that is the spark of hope, fear, life and death. It is within his mind to live, die, weep and rejoice. If he would live, *he lives not for himself.*

This master marker upon the endless page of time, idyllic dreamer, rhyme-scheme composer, *knows* that you and he are one and what is good for him must be good for you, and that which is not good, takes from him that which he would have, share and be—to you.

By prodigious effort of vision, we create. Yet how difficult to claim credit for ourselves! While creativeness appears to lack connecting links from past to present—from another man, another mind, or another time—the aspiration of longing souls has spent genius in giving to me what I may call "my own." I create only because I also have been beckoned by the elusive, constant, and ever-changing, from one time, person, place, element, or idea—

always different and yet the same. Beyond this vision created *is a spirit creative.*

The analysis is only partial. What any man would have—*he has!* What I would be—*I am!* What you would receive—*you must give!* What we would give—*we have received!*

We would be saved? By whom? For what? By every man we meet—by every deed—by every seeking quest. We would be saved by whom, for what? By the thoughts of our minds—by the hopes of other men; that you and I, and he and she, and we and they can be more together than alone.

YOUR ASSIGNMENT FOR THIS WEEK

Commit to memory and relate to your daily life: *"As the hart panteth after the water brooks, So panteth my soul after thee, O God. My soul thirsteth for God, for the living God." —Psalm 42:1-2. " . . a man shall be as a hiding-place from the wind, and a covert from the tempest, as streams of water in a dry place, as the shade of a great rock in a weary land. And the eyes of them that see shall not be dim, and the ears of them that hear shall hearken." —Isaiah 32:1-3.*

A further consideration: The man seeking gold has the greatest need for gold, and the determination to find that which he seeks. The man who seeks new worlds to conquer has a need to meet and makes the challenge of a new world. The one who would stand on a mountain top needs to lift himself above the valley floor. *The one who would be one with God, IS one with God, and with his fellow man.*
He has determined life—more than appearance.
He has challenged and conquered that which overwhelms a lesser man.
He's found the "gold of life," a new world in the gift of love. He's stood where only vision "sees beyond the now." Perhaps, with a subtle awareness he has sustained himself and others with what he sought.

And now: Step by step we proceed along the path of our own choosing. Where will it lead? To the turning point of a self-directed goal? Or to words, and words, and words, and thoughts, and dreams, and visions—and hope without hope—because we expected others to do that which we must do? Dream big dreams! Chart your course! Set your sails! Your helmsman is the spirit within, without, and around you! *"I will instruct thee and teach thee in the way which thou shalt go." —Psalm 32:8*

MAKE THIS—

YOUR DAILY AFFIRMATION FOR THE WEEK:

"I would be saved? By whom? For what? I would be saved by an embodiment of knowledge without limitation, by the capacity I have to be more than I have been, for a contradiction of appearances and a decree of the doctrine by which I would live."

Your basis of reality in today's living

The starting point of every act, thought and feeling lies solely within my mind. Nothing outside me, absolutely nothing, has power to harm, hinder, or help me except and unless the power of my mind welcomes it in warm embrace. I would be saved? By whom? For what? I would be saved by the harmony of life and my perception that I must relate to life. And "life," in its simplest reduction of awareness, is that I must concern myself with more than me. By whom? By everything! By everyone! For life is animate in the most inanimate of objects through my response of drawing near or forcing away; I give life to all I see. For What? For the darkness I can dispel, the beauty I bring forth in that which others may behold as unsightly, without beauty, unloveliness. I would be saved? By whom? For what? *I would be saved by an embodiment of knowledge without limitation. By the capacity I have to be more than I have been, for a contradiction of appearances and a decree of the doctrine by which I would live!*

A thought to think upon—The thoughts within my mind are only those which I have embraced, accepted, and nurtured—the conditions of my affairs are the results of that which I have given thought to. There are "greener pastures" other than where you now stand. These visions are within your mind; this "grazing land," within your effort.

Question 1. is an assignment. Definiteness of purpose and "inner faith," nurtured by a burning desire, produce far more than the limitation of appearance. *While not trying to pick a goal that will change your life, pick one with definiteness of purpose. It will change your life!* Set a time for its accomplishment and the means you will use to get it.

Assignment 2. No form of human exchange approximates pure benefit as much as an idea communicated. One with awareness expressed this aptly: "If I give you one of my dollars in return for one of yours, each of us will have no more than he started with; but, if I give you a thought in return for one of your thoughts, each of us will have gained 100 percent dividend on his investment of time." *Write down an idea you believe would be worth sharing with others—and then share it with others.*

Assignment 3. *Write down words of force, power, meaning, and motive that will stimulate your thinking to emulate, in body, mind, and spirit, the words you have chosen. Example: "Thunder-ing waterfall" (Life, vitality, movement, and beauty). "The peaceful lake" (calm, strength, substance, sustenance and purpose). Now that you have written them down, imprint them upon your mind. Think them! Feel them! Act them! Be them!*

Question 4. As the single drop of water is part of all the water in the world, each man, although part of the whole, is individual. *In reference to what has just been stated, how best can you express true individuality?*

Question 5. From deep within man's heart there issues forth a truth. Rising to the surface, this truth becomes a question—"True or false?" *In a simple, acceptable statement, why should truth contain doubt?*

"These things write we unto you, that your joy may be full."
—I John 1:14

"STIMULATORS TO ACTION"—

The caption itself is alive with motive for movement!
—"STIMULATORS TO ACTION!" "Stimulate";
encourage; impel;
rouse to activity or heightened action.

"To"; toward; approach; a rise to power;
in contact with; reaching as far as.
"Action"; life; energy; intent; purpose!
To which we can well add: "strong, vigorous,
full of life, animated, ebullient, fervent!"
Any one of these action adjectives, clasped to your bosom,
will STIMULATE YOU TO ACTION!
"The word of God is quick, and powerful."
—Hebrews 7:16

How to Pray for Practical Purposes

The *"manna"* of prayer is the result of correct effort, diligently pursued, as the result or consequence of prayer. The *"manner"* of prayer is harmonious accord with spiritual principles, producing an outcome in harmony with man and nature. Thus it becomes necessary for most of us to change our thinking about many aspects of the world and our part in it so that we comprehend what will produce positive rather than negative results.

Manna has been called *"The bread of life," "the Word of God," and "realization."* The most varying emotions preside over what we consider ours and how we shall get "the bread of life." The human mind creates images and perspectives to gain favor and attain prosperity. Health, peace of mind, and relatedness appear to be in a different category. Again, man becomes the dupe of misapplication. *There is but one truth! There are two concepts of truth: correct comprehension and false understanding.*

Translation of thought into rewarding results requires a higher level of consciousness than thought of self alone. Here we witness translation into transformation. There is an awareness that *all* things—health, peace of mind, prosperity, and good—are ours now; that these particulars do not necessitate struggle. We are bid to incorporate into our way of life a pattern of thinking, with full realization that our thought is *"The formulating process of mind,"* and that thoughts are *vibrant, moving, directing processes forming and shaping according to the thinker of the thought."* How we arrive at realization is by recognizing that the principle producing desired ends is exactly the same, under all conditions and in every circumstance, for every man and woman on the face of this earth.

Here we encounter difficulty. One may look upon his fellow

man as blessed or gifted, and upon himself as restricted to the imprisoning environment of the narrow world in which he finds himself. If this is so, a new perspective of self and others is in order.

YOUR ASSIGNMENT FOR THIS WEEK

Set the stage. Prepare your mind to both receive and give—by finding a place of quiet. Give no thought to your mind, body, or affairs. Be still.

Realization can only evolve as one seeks to break the chains binding one to a narrow, personal, individual world. Revelation expands the significant unity of the whole.

This day: A profound experience awaits you as you make a genuine effort to encompass that which you would reject. *Perform a task you could avoid; serve someone you may not like; contribute to that from which you would withdraw; share a spiritual truth with someone—but know this as a living truth in your own life first.*

Know: That where you are *is* holy ground *and all is holy. Be observant of the obligations you would impose on others. Make an honest effort to see in everything a Godlike quality. What you observe will be a reflection of what you are.*

Extend your vision beyond the narrow confines of where you are to where and what you would be. There is but one worthy aim in life—to know God—and in knowing God, being that which you seek.

Now: Meditate upon the following scripture:

"He that hath an ear, let him hear what the Spirit saith to the churches. To him that overcometh, to him will I give of the hidden manna, and I will give him a white stone, and upon the stone a new name written, which no one knoweth but he that receiveth it." —Revelation 2:17

MAKE THIS—

YOUR DAILY AFFIRMATION FOR THE WEEK:

"For this one day I make a genuine effort to adhere to principles of truth. Each thought is positive, prayerful, kind, loving, and sharing. I involve myself meaningfully, saying and doing nothing that in any way denigrates me or another."

Your basis of reality
in today's living

In consideration of the admonition to *"Do unto others as ye would have them do unto you,"* we receive as we give. This is the "Manna and the manner of prayer." However prone we are to relate this (in our words, although seldom in our actions) to individuals, doing unto others as we would have them do unto us involves every area of life. We are working with the principle that "like attracts like." Life can only return that which we give to life. When our thoughts are constructive, the ideas evolving will not be constrictive. The object of thought becomes the image of reality. *Know* that the *"Manna is the manner of prayer."* Faith, hope, health, prosperity, peace of mind, abundance, and doing good are good words. Incorporate them into your manner of prayer—they are *"the Manna of prayer."*

> "For this one day I make a genuine effort to adhere to principles of truth. Each thought is powerfully positive, prayerful, kind, loving, and sharing. I involve myself meaningfully."
> "Meditate upon these things; give thyself wholly to them."
> —I Timothy 4:15

The task ahead—

That which lies ahead at any moment of your experience or mine can be a hard task-master or the employment of a fruit-bearing lesson in living. Which it is depends on us. Life can be a process of meaning and significant goals. Accept the challenge. The benefit will be more than salutory.

Your self-development questions

Question 1. In the book of Luke, Chapter eight, verse 18, we read: *"For whosoever hath, to him shall be given."* Recognizing the importance of having good, powerful, positive and productive ideas, we can readily ascertain that these are productive of good, powerful, positive and productive results. We can also discern that anything in our mind that is less than positive, spiritual, or productive will produce the same. *List several ideas that are to be the "well-spring" of greater good in your life this coming week.*

Question 2. Spiritual progress is defined by Charles Fillmore as "Growth in the conception and expression of spiritual ideas." *What does this mean?*

Question 3. Most of us are always ready, willing, and able to come up with the right answer to another's problem. *If someone had a healing need, a need for prosperity, and a need for peace of mind, how specifically, would you have him pray?*
Do you pray in this manner? If not, why not?

"I will pray with the spirit, and I will pray with the understanding also." —I Thessalonians 5:17

"STIMULATORS TO ACTION"—

Pick a distinct and distant goal.
One that seems far beyond your reach.
Now write upon a piece of paper and on
your mind, heart, and soul the worthiness of that
goal.
Then—
Ask yourself this question: "Am I worthy?"
If you are—
You will achieve the goal!

WEEKLY PROGRAM
NUMBER
50

How to Achieve Your
Self-Directed Destiny

The purpose of any course of study is to enlighten, broaden, and give the individual and his life breadth, depth, and meaning. The purpose of learning is knowledge. Knowledge, in its right application, is wisdom.

At the end of each day there may be cause to reflect upon the benefits of that particular day. What course you have taken becomes the cause of the course you will pursue—unless that which you have learned brings you to avoid that which is to be avoided.

At the end of the day, will there be an unprogrammed recollection of much that you could have done and did not do? Or will there be an unbroken course relating to every circumstance and individual in such manner that only good will come forth for you and him?

In the Book of Genesis, Chapter 13, verses 14, 15, and 17, we are admonished to *"Lift up now thine eyes, and look from the place where thou art, northward and southward and eastward and westward: for all the land which thou seest, to thee will I give it, and to thy seed for ever. Arise, walk through the land in the length of it and in the breadth of it; for unto thee will I give it."* We are free to read into these words what we will. However their truth is carried across centuries, to another time and place, into your life and mine. What is this truth? How do we find it?

YOUR ASSIGNMENT FOR THIS WEEK

First: *Know* there is nothing esoteric about any of the words of wisdom given in the Bible. These teachings were not designed to be understood by the specially initiated alone. There is nothing private nor secret in this book of impulse and revelation. These inspired writings and their many meanings are open to all who would receive.

Second: *Know that while you have the option to embrace these truths, you repudiate them when you reject them.* Are we not left without an excuse when we fail to observe landmarks left behind by those who have gone before?

Now: As there are untold colors, hues, tints, and shadings from each color, assent to the possibility of myriad meanings applicable to every problem, challenge, and path set before you—for each is a path set before you.

It may seem strange to find a message related to life and its living in the giving away of land. But read again Chapter 13 of the book of Genesis, verses 14, through 17. Read and digest them *word by word.* Ponder them. You will *"Arise, walk through the land in the length of it and in the breadth of it."*

Make a daily habit of applying the truth of your new vision.

> "I have heard of thee by the hearing of the ear: but now mine eye seeth thee." —Job 42:5

> "Thou visitest the earth, and waterest it: thou greatly enrichest it with the river of God." —Psalm 65:9

> "My eyes shall behold the land that is far off."—Isaiah 33:17

A moment of silence: *"In quietness and in Trust."* —Isaiah 30:15

MAKE THIS—

YOUR DAILY AFFIRMATION FOR THE WEEK:

"Look from the place where thou art." —Genesis 13:14

"I am always in the presence of God! Whatever the circumstance, condition, person, time, or place—I am ever in the presence of God!"

Your basis of reality in today's living

We who are living recognize the importance of a breath of air or a bite of food as part of our ability to continue to live. We can, in reality, say, "These are necessary for man to live—and are of great worth."

Our greatest possession is without price—our *inner life*.

At the end of each day I may look back and question, wonder, or know what I may have accomplished or not accomplished. *I can look from the place where Thou art. I can always look from the time, place, circumstance, and condition and know that as I look at man or meaning, bad or good—"I can look from the place where Thou art!"* Though we are forward looking creatures we can go in only one direction at a time. How much is life like a game of checkers! We move forward and back, and to one side or the other. This is fine in a game of checkers. Seldom do we make progress in life except when we move in the direction of that goal toward which we have set our sights. *The next move is yours!*

Your self-development questions

Question 1. So often we hear the cry, "Why has this happened to me?" It appears this is the time one turns to truth—to God. *What do you believe to be the greatest influence you could exert in your own life and in the lives of others, to use truth at all times?*

Question 2. It has been said, "Man must love and be loved if he is to live beyond existence." *List a different way in which you can be more loving each day of this coming week.*

Question 3. Whatever we accept in our mind becomes a reality to us. *How can we accept only that which is for our highest good?* If you tell me to "turn to God," I will ask, *"How does one turn to God, and turn to God in every situation?*

Question 4. Many of the things we "see" in our mind do not exist except within the mind. Yet everything we see, hold, feel, and touch came from Divine Mind or man's mind. *How would you proceed to "create" an idea to better your world and to bring it to fruition? Do you have a valid reason for not doing it? If so, give the reason.*

"All men shall . . .declare the work of God" Psalm 64:9

"STIMULATORS TO ACTION"—

Precisely because you are an individual,
you have complete control over your own thoughts.

"Choose you this day whom you will serve."

"A pattern to them which should hereafter believe."
> *1 Timothy 1:16*

"By love serve one another."
> *—Galatians 5:13*

*"Though I be free from all men, yet have I made
myself servant unto all."*
> *—I Corinthians 9:19*

"God hath from the beginning chosen you . . . "
> *—2 Thessalonians 2:13*

"Choose you this day whom ye will serve."
> *—Joshua 24:15*

WEEKLY PROGRAM

NUMBER

51

Now that You've Prayed—What?

As I look upon a tree I see a thousand things: the tree itself, the form and fashion of man and God, a thing of beauty, shade, shelter, and sustenance. Beyond the guise of wood, bark, leaf, and limb I behold far more than sheltering shade—I see life in glorious splendor!

We cannot precisely measure what man will relate to, how or by what means. We can know that the object viewed, is in essence, what it is. Perspective makes it neither more or less. We cannot behold that which does not exist—except within our mind.

I see what vision cannot see—the thought: "What have YOU seen as I and others passed your way?"

Now that you have prayed—what?

Do you see what eyes alone observe, or are you now obliged by that which has touched you to "touch" reality, and know with all that you are kindred? *Kindred! One! This is what! Now that you've prayed!*

YOUR ASSIGNMENT FOR THIS WEEK

Commit to memory: *"For both he that sanctifieth and they who are sanctified are all of one . . . "* —*Hebrews 2:11*

Read, each day, the following scripture:

" . . . I beseech you, . . . show courage . . . be bold against some, who count of us as if we walked according to the flesh. For though we walk in the flesh, we do not war according to the flesh for the weapons of our warfare are not of the flesh, but mighty before God to . . . casting down imaginations, and every high thing that is exalted against the knowledge of God . . . reckon this . . . we are not to number . . . ourselves with them that . . . measure themselves by themselves, and comparing themselves with themselves, are without understanding. . . . but according to the measure of the province which God apportioned to us as a measure to reach even unto you."

—II Corinthians 10

Now: During this coming week and *for the remainder of your life*, with everything *you look upon—relate!* No effort is required to ascertain dissimilarity—we have spent a lifetime doing this. *Seek similarities. Relate!*

Fashion an allegation that will ascertain itself only in application and performance.

MAKE THIS—

YOUR DAILY AFFIRMATION FOR THE WEEK:

"I have come this far by faith! I now proceed in the certain knowledge that steps taken have produced. I shall continue to evolve as I persevere in daily incorporating an awareness of the importance of spiritual principles in my life."

Your basis of reality in today's living

"Prayer is an attitude of mind—a posture of being."

Perceiving that attitudes have improved and acknowledging that amended attitudes ameliorate unwanted conditions, it is reasonable that I now ponder: *"Now that you've prayed—what?"*

Now that I've prayed I know and expect to be the recipient of the dynamics of living. My expectation is the anticipation of knowing.

"I have come this far by faith! I shall continue to evolve as I persevere in daily incorporating an awareness of the importance of spiritual principles in my life."

Your self-development questions

Question 1. The power of prayer empowers one to live a far different life because one who prays has changed. *In the light of the sense in which prayer has been presented, define your new perspective of prayer.*

Question 2. *Now that you've prayed—WHAT? Write it out in cold facts!*

Question 3. The poet renders impact, meaning, vividness and awakened sense from the spirit of what he senses. His is celebration of the world, its moods and memory in a living experience for those who would live. *In each man's heart and soul there is the "poetry of the soul" to be laid bare and shared. You have had deeper thoughts than others know. Please write them down, and then share them with others.*

Question 4. There are two realities: 1) the ultimate reality and, 2) the reality of confusion of the individual as he encounters that which is unmistakable, evident, and unequivocal; i.e., that we must love to be loved; that we must give to receive. *"For as he thinketh in his heart, so is he." —Proverbs 23:7. Contemplate how you will embrace the "ultimate reality" in your way of life.*

"Now that you've prayed—what?"

"Teach me thy way, O Lord, that I may walk in thy truth." —Psalm 86:11. "Let us hear the conclusion of the whole matter: Fear [love] God, and keep his commandments: for this is the whole duty of man." —Ecclesiastes 12:13. "Then shalt thou walk in thy way safely, and thy foot shall not stumble." —Proverbs 3:23. "We have a building of God, an house not made with hands." —2 Corinthians 5:1. "I have chosen you, and ordained you, that ye should go and bring forth fruit." —John 15:16. " . . . thou shalt be in league with the stones of the field . . . and shall be at peace . . . Lo this, we have searched it, so it is; Hear it, and know thou it for thy good." —Job 5:23, 27. "Approving ourselves as the ministers of God, . . . By pureness, by knowledge, . . . by kindness, . . . by love unfeigned." —2 Corinthians 6:4, 6.

"STIMULATORS TO ACTION"—

1. Give thought to what will make tomorrow a better day.
2. Write it down.
3. Consider your part.
4. Seriously consider the next question.
5. Why wait until tomorrow?

WEEKLY PROGRAM
NUMBER
52

How to Measure Your Progress Using These Weekly Programs

All of us, at one period of our life or another, have stood upon the shifting sands of time and shore and gazed across distant water at the far horizon. To one on a ship, looking toward the shore upon which we stood, there would not be an awareness that we were part of their distant horizon.

At some time or other most of us have stood on mountain top and looked off into the distance. We beheld a far different horizon. On the horizon may have been mountain peaks forming not a thin straight line like the seashore, but an uneven, jagged mixture of tones and colors, seeming to blend the sky and land. If the horizon was far away, it may have been difficult to determine where mountains ended and sky began. If we stood on a valley floor and looked at surrounding mountains, certainly our horizon would be considerably narrowed. Our physical horizon had a visible beginning and end. But at this moment, the horizon of our spirit is elevated and extends beyond, to the majesty of the mountains and the grandeur of God's handiwork.

As you look out upon the ocean from a ship, you know that there is much beyond the horizon that you see. *There is an ever-continuing horizon beyond where we are.*

Far horizons and distant goals seem to be the lot of many who pray. An idea enters the mind: "It is health I want!" and the intricacies of how to be healthy obscure the magic, meaning, and miracle of bodily well-being. *They remain sick, and that which was sought becomes a far distant goal.* The only horizon looming large and intimate is the illness, problem, or condition you are trying to

270

get rid of. The image you *had* in your mind drifts off into infinity. The thought of "well-being" becomes a tiny speck—disappearing in disillusionment. *By what means is one to pray?*

By what means is one to pray? Whatever you seek, look no farther than where you are. For where you are *is* holy ground! Where you are is the makeup and medley of life. Where you are is the problem! But in tranquility is the unifying mood and the healing awareness. Where you are *is* the means to determine the end. *"Yes, but how do I apply lofty-sounding words to down-to-earth problems?"* Look no farther than where you are—and then look far beyond wherever you are. Observe your problem for what it is, and from where you are. Perhaps you know you are sick and you want health. If someone guaranteed you $100,000 one year from now, providing you saved *$1000,* you would *find,* not look for—*but find*—a thousand ways to make that *$1000,* no matter how difficult it may have been in the past to have saved anything.

Health, peace of mind, prosperity, friends, happiness, and well-being are worth the effort. Within the illness, problem, or need, the solution is there to be revealed. *But we have to be determined to have health come hell or high water. We have to more than want to have friends. Our desire must, here and now, motivate us into friendship.* This is true of whatever we would have.

The most violent of storms, the hurricane, has in its very center a place of calm, aptly called the "eye." Somewhere deep within the problem, the person, need, hope, fear, or frustration is the *"I"*—that which is the means, the method, and the answer. We need no elaborate words to elicit it. The significance of attaining health—releasing ourselves from the view that the solution we seek is far away and by other means contains all the elements of life, all that which awakens us to that which has been felt in moments of inspiration or desperation. If we want hot water, we heat the water we have. We don't look for someone to exchange hot water for cold. Our problems have a kinship with a prison cell: we can be enclosed, encompassed, restrained, and shackled by the problem itself. Our vision is circumscribed within the narrow confines of a limited perspective. Whatever we seek seems far away—a far horizon and a distant goal.

You would have health? An answer to your prayer? A purpose to your life? *Has your mind been provoked to thought? Let your spirit be stimulated to action!* Join with me on a journey of the mind.

YOUR ASSIGNMENT FOR THIS WEEK

Assume a comfortable position.

Close your eyes. Relax! You are on a plane. Far below, the water is bluish green—far different than it appears when beheld from below.

The trees appear different—not like trees at all, but like a ruffed bit of paint on an unreal sea. The plane lands. You walk upon the sands of silent time, shifting imperceptively from where you were to where you are—

From where you are to where you would be,

 From disquiet to peace,

  From illness to wholeness,

   From want to fullness,

    From insouciance to awareness,

     From unknowing to certainty.

"Where I am is holy ground! Where I am is where I seek to be!"

In closing, may this be the opening and the beginning—

The meaning of "God's will"

You ask "How do I know what is God's will for me?" . . . This is a searching question I have often asked myself. It is a question that has been asked before by men and women seeking to know God in a more meaningful way.

We all look for this thread that must be woven into the fabric of our life, and yet, though the pattern is with us all the time, too often we fail to recognize that which we seek. We look for ways of living, thinking, and expression that will broaden our horizon, and

listen for a sound that will tell us "Here is the value of life; this is
the dawn, the day, and a new beginning."

Few of us approach anything from exactly the same starting
point, and dogmas and doctrines can obscure that which we seek
to unfold within ourselves.

To answer your question, I shall attempt not so much to tell
you things as to share with you feelings I have, in the hope that
that which you can experience will mean more to you than words
convey. However, I shall share some thoughts and insights.

What we seek to know, in "knowing God's will for us," is never
static—it is a growing, changing education of the soul from within
each individual. God's will for us is not a changing will, but as we
evolve in consciousness, we change from what we appear to be, to
what we were meant to be. God's will for us is like a forming
cloud which takes form, shape, beauty. Building high, expanding,
and growing, the cloud is beautiful, powerful, and useful. From
lake, river, and pond, the cloud gathers unto itself drops of
moisture that will become substance to fulfill man's needs. Like
the cloud, we shall grow in beauty, power, and usefulness,
gathering unto ourselves the abundance of God which will become
substance to supply our needs and those of others.

God's will for man is the reason for his being and the object of
his existence. The object of each man's existence is to demonstrate
the truth of being. Through relating we demonstrate truth as a
living experience. We learn this truth in one of two ways: first, by
knowledge and application; and second, by eventual consequences
of lack of discernment.

We now have a starting point. Beginning with the destination,
with the recognition of a governing law, let us continue our quest.
Presuming that I have established the existence of God in my life,
I must then accept that God's will for me is good.

"How do I know what is God's will for me?" There are many
ways. There is a quality of knowing within man that tells him the
truth of a thing, though he may not find the words to convey that
which he knows. Knowing God's will is something felt rather than
stated, Something experienced rather than reasoned.

I've come a long way and I still have not answered your
question. The Psalmist said, "Be still, and know ... " —Psalm

46:10. And He who taught us much said, "And I say unto you, ask, and it shall be given to you; seek, and ye shall find; knock, and it shall be opened unto you."—Luke 11:9.

We can know the answer to our question by heeding the words and wisdom of Him who lived long ago and far away. We can know by seeking to "know" in meditation, when we enter the Silence. We can begin in trust, proceed in faith, and know in moments when we still the mind and body. We can know the will of God when we become still, and when we listen, believe, and accept the words of Him who has showed The Way.